Impact of Globalisation on Tribals

Impact of Globalisation on Tribals

In the Context of Kerala

Mathew Aerthayil

Published in association with
Indian Social Institute, Bangalore

RAWAT PUBLICATIONS
Jaipur • New Delhi • Bangalore • Mumbai • Hyderabad • Guwahati

ISBN 81-316-0233-8

Published by
Prem Rawat for **Rawat Publications**
Satyam Apts, Sector 3, Jawahar Nagar, Jaipur 302 004 (India)
Phone: 0141 265 1748 / 7006 Fax: 0141 265 1748
E-mail: info@rawatbooks.com
Website: www.rawatbooks.com

New Delhi Office
4858/24, Ansari Road, Daryaganj, New Delhi 110 002
Phone: 011 2326 3290

Also at Bangalore, Mumbai, Hyderabad and Guwahati

Typeset by Rawat Computers, Jaipur
Printed at Chaman Enterprises, New Delhi

Contents

Abbreviations

AGMS	:	Adivasi Gothra Maha Sabha
APL	:	Above Poverty Line
BPL	:	Below Poverty Line
CPI(M)	:	Communist Party of India (Marxist)
FYP	:	Five-Year Plan
GATT	:	General Agreement on Tariff and Trade
IMF	:	International Monetary Fund
ITDP	:	Integrated Tribal Development Project
NEP	:	New Economic Policy
NGO	:	Non-Government Organisation
NPPO	:	Non-Party Political Organisation
MLA	:	Member of Legislative Assembly
MNC	:	Multi-National Corporation
MRTP	:	Monopoly Restriction and Trade Practice Act
PDS	:	Public Distribution System
PHC	:	Public Health Centre

SAP	:	Structural Adjustment Programme
SHG	:	Self-Help Groups
TNC	:	Trans-National Corporation
TRIP	:	Trade Related Aspects of Intellectual Property Rights
WB	:	World Bank
WTO	:	World Trade Organisation

List of Tables

Preface

After India adopted the path of globalisation in the 1990s, many positive changes have happened in our country. Among other things India has become one of the fastest growing economies in the world and a leading country in information technology. But on the human development index, India is ranked as one of the lowest in the world. This means there is a contradiction in our development paradigm. As the government itself has admitted in different ways, the fruit of our development has not reached the majority of the people, especially farmers and marginalised groups like Dalits and tribals. Has our positive economic development negatively affected these groups? As serious discussion is going on in our country about this crucial problem it is relevant to study the effect of globalisation on various sections of our common people. It was with this aim that I thought of making a study on the impact of globalisation on tribals in Kerala, the most backward and marginalised section of the population in the state. The immediate context of this study is my own contact with the tribals in Kerala through the outreach training programmes of Indian Social Institute, Bangalore (ISI), and my witnessing their plight during the last few years. The objective was to examine how the process of globalisation has affected the life of the tribals.

The study has analysed the impact of globalisation on the livelihood of tribals in Kerala including their employment and availability of essential commodities, and on their sociocultural life including their cultural and religious practices, health, education and tribal women. The first part of the book gives a comprehensive description about the socioeconomic and cultural situation of tribals in Kerala particularly their land alienation and their organisational struggle for land. Since the study has found some negative impact of globalisation on the life of the tribals, the last chapter gives a few suggestions and strategies to counter the impact of globalisation on tribals, which could be taken up by the government and social and tribal organisations for the development of the tribals in Kerala.

I undertook this study as a member of the staff of Indian Social Institute, Bangalore, and the Institute sponsored this research project. Many people have helped me in this study. Mr. Baiju K.K. who, as the Research Assistant of the study, did most of the work in the first part of the research namely, preparing the questionnaire and coordinating the data collection and tabulation. I thank him for his dedicated and determined work, but for which this study would not have been possible. I acknowledge gratefully the services of many investigators including tribals and non-tribals who did the data collection for this study. I thank the social scientists and members of the ISI academic staff, who gave constructive suggestions on the draft report. I gratefully remember the Directors and staff of TUDI, VOICE and JVALA who helped me to make the background arrangement for this research. I am thankful to the tribal men and women who contributed towards this study. My sincere thanks go to Fr. Richard Sequeira S.J., who did the language editing of the text. I thank Ms. Vimala Mathews for neatly and carefully doing the secretarial work for the report. Finally I express my gratitude to Rawat Publications for accepting this work for publication.

Mathew Aerthayil

1

Globalisation and Tribals in Kerala: Issues and Methodology

It was with police firing on Adivasis at Muthanga, in Wayanad district, Kerala, that the problems of tribals in Kerala were highlighted at the national level. Land was the basic problem of Adivasis, for which they had been agitating for many years. It culminated in the occupation of the Wild Life Sanctuary at Muthanga leading to police firing and death of an Adivasi and a policeman.

Land, though a very important and basic problem of the Adivasis in Kerala, is not their only problem. Other problems emanated from land alienation which adversely affected their livelihood and culture. Later, these Adivasis became victims of exploitation and oppression at the hands of landlords, settlers and even the government. Now, they have become the most marginalised group in Kerala. As a result, in recent years, they have been facing acute unemployment problem resulting in starvation and even starvation death. The standard of education, health and food security of Adivasis seems to be deteriorating and their culture is also getting destroyed. It can be assumed that these problems are related to the policy of globalisation adopted by the Government of India.

India adopted the process of globalisation and drastically changed its socioeconomic policies based on the guidelines and requirements of World Trade Organisation (WTO). About fifteen years after the process started India has become one of the fastest growing economies in the world. Its growth in information technology has become world famous. Yet the vast majority of the people including the farmers and marginalised groups like tribals and Dalits do not seem to have benefited from globalisation; rather their lives seem to have deteriorated as a result of the neo-liberal policies. Therefore, the question can be raised whether there is any relationship between the situation of the tribals and the present economic policies based on globalisation. How have the liberalisation and privatisation that go with globalisation affected the means of livelihood, health, and the religious and cultural practices of the tribals? Are the tribal women particularly affected by the changes in the socioeconomic policy of the country? How can the tribals face the challenges of globalisation? In short, this study examines whether the tribals in Kerala, who were already facing myriads of problems, have been affected by the process of globalisation and whether their lives have become more vulnerable as a result of globalisation. It is important to understand how the new economic policy of globalisation affects the tribals so that the government and the tribals themselves can adopt remedial measures.

Objectives of the Study

General

To find out the impact of globalisation on tribals of Kerala.

Specific

1. To examine the life and problems of tribals in Kerala.
2. To study the impact of globalisation on the livelihood of the tribals including employment, wages and availability of essential commodities.
3. To explore the impact of globalisation on the sociocultural life, health and education of the tribals in Kerala.
4. To suggest alternative strategies for tribals to face the challenges of globalisation.

Globalisation in India

Globalisation is an international phenomenon which has swept through every country in the world. India, too, adopted this system mainly for its economic growth and development. Globalisation is affecting all sections of people either positively or negatively. Its nature is so vast and varied that there is need to specify the areas which are taken up in relation to this study. Therefore, this section explains some of the basic features of globalisation as adopted in India, which can have a bearing on the life of the tribals.

Though global movement of capital and labour existed hundreds of years back it probably expressed itself most powerfully when imperialist countries captured global markets as well as colonies. Once the British made India its colony, it imposed its own laws and governing system to perpetuate its dominance over the country. These laws included those related to land, forest and industry, which affected the people of India, especially the marginalised people like the Dalits and the tribals, adversely.

Globalisation is "a process which involves growing economic interdependence of countries worldwide" (Singh, 1998: 3). Singh emphasises the economic integration, interrelationship and interdependence of countries. This relationship is specified by Oommen, when he defines it as "a process of transnationalisation of capital, production and even consumer tastes and preferences on a single global logic of exchange" (Oommen, 1993: 9). Capital, production and consumption are internationalised based on exchange of goods and services. Globalisation of finance through capital investment in stock exchanges is an important part of globalisation. Thus globalisation can be said to involve five major factors: rapid growth in international financial transactions, fast growth in trade especially among Trans-National Corporations (TNCs), surge in foreign direct investment largely contributed by TNCs, the emergence of global markets, and the diffusion of technologies and ideas through rapid expansion of a globalised transportation and communication system (Singh, 1998).

The background of the present-day globalisation in India was prepared in 1980 when India took a five billion dollar loan from International Monetary Fund (IMF) with all its conditionalities. But globalisation of economy in the strict sense probably started in 1991 with the New Economic Policy (NEP) based on the Structural

Adjustment Programme (SAP) as proposed by the World Bank and the IMF. The present study uses the term 'globalisation' in the sense of a phenomenon started in India mainly in the 1990s. Based on the SAP the following were some of the changes brought about in Indian economy:

Trade Liberalisation

Trade liberalisation means elimination of import quotas and reduction in quantitative and qualitative restrictions on import and export according to the guidelines of the World Trade Organisation (WTO). It is meant to facilitate free trade and free movements of goods and services among the countries across the globe, which is an important aspect of globalisation. To achieve this India has adopted several measures including reduction in tariffs and customs, elimination of state monopoly on import and export, simplification of Foreign Exchange Regulation Act (FERA), convertibility of rupee within a time framework and free movement of financial capital.

One important trade rule that the WTO enforced was of patent laws. The new rules on patent were included in the Trade-Related Aspects of Intellectual Property Rights (TRIPS). According to these rules, patent protection rights for products for 14 to 20 years along with protection for trade marks, copyrights and other intellectual property rights were enforced. These rules were in favour of Trans-National Corporations (TNCs) as their products had to be protected from the cheaper rivals from the poor countries. One example is sale of pharmaceuticals made from the copies of patent technology. Multi-National Corporations (MNCs) who had patent for these products challenged the production of cheap HIV/AIDS drugs made available by developing countries to poor countries of Africa, though they did not succeed in it. According to these patent rules, genetic materials in the form of traditional seeds or plant life evolved over generations by farmers and tribals are not patentable, as they belong to the "common heritage of mainkind" to be shared by all including the developed countries, while genetically modified seeds or plant life will get patent protection. Some MNCs have patented basmati rice and the process of extracting medical substance from Indian Neem trees, which were known to farmers in India for long. Thus, the TRIP rules could play havoc with traditional plants and medicines of tribals.

As a result of liberalisation, industrial and consumer goods were freely imported into the country. Agricultural products in which India is self-sufficient too, were imported in large quantities and varieties, resulting in the crash in prices of local agricultural products. When the farmers did not get remunerative prices for their products, a crisis occurred, and one expression of this was the increasing incidence of suicide among farmers, as was reported from Karnataka, Andhra Pradesh, Maharashtra and Kerala. The crisis was deeper in Kerala as the price of most of the agricultural crops, especially the cash crops, crashed to an abysmally low level. This had an adverse effect on tribals as they were very much dependent on agriculture. This study tries to examine the impact of liberalisation as part of globalisation on tribals in Kerala.

Privatisation

Privatisation is a basic component of globalisation. The New Industrial Policy enunciated in 1991 based on NEP brought about the following changes:

1. Transfer of public enterprises to private sector. This could be done either by selling enterprises to private companies or by selling shares to the public or by stopping funds for them instead of allowing them to raise funds from the market.
2. Encouraging private sector to invest in industries with greater freedom than in earlier times. This is done by elimination of licensing and control, deregulation of prices of goods and services, and removal of restrictions on merger under Monopology Restriction and Trade Practice (MRTP) Act. Besides, private sector is allowed to be controlled by market forces and competition.

When many public sector industries were privatised, the scope of employment for SCs/STs through reservation was reduced considerably. To make industries efficient, the government changed its labour policy thus curtailing certain rights of the workers. The new policy has adversely affected the marginalised sections. Deregulation of prices of essential commodities also directly and adversely affected the weaker sections. In addition, Public Distribution System (PDS) of the country was almost dismantled on the line of globalisation through reclassification of beneficiaries and raising prices of the commodities sold in fair price shops. This was done to reduce government subsidy on essential food commodities. The vulnerable sections who depended heavily on ration shops and civil supplies found it difficult to buy essential commodities at a higher price as their purchasing power got reduced due to low employment opportunities. As a result, the intake of food grains from the PDS drastically declined throughout India during the last few years. This study will look into the effect of privatisation as part of globalisation, on the tribals in Kerala.

Privatisation also means giving permission for foreign investment in many industries. This is an important feature of globalisation since TNCs, especially from developed countries, invest in developing countries, facilitating flow of foreign capital and technology across countries. As part of the globalisation process, three sectors in Indian economy were opened up phase by phase to foreign capital: Basic metals, heavy chemicals and machinery in the first phase, telecommunication, oil and gas in the second phase, and financial sector, ports and internal transport in the final stage. The aim was to increase foreign exchange reserve and to modernise these sectors to make them efficient and competitive in the international market.

As MNCs and TNCs generally produce luxury and non-essential consumer goods for middle class and the rich, the marginalised groups like Dalits and tribals are excluded from the production process and its fruits. Besides, as foreign companies do not produce essential goods needed for ordinary people, marginalised sections are not able to benefit from the high growth rate of the national economy. Foreign Direct Investment in tourism, transport and mining can often deprive tribals of their natural resources like land and forest.

Withdrawal of Government from Social Sectors Like Education and Health

According to the requirements of World Trade Organisation (WTO), World Bank and International Monetary Fund (IMF), the Government of India started reducing its spending in many areas, especially in social sectors. This was done by reducing subsidy to agriculture, small scale industries and the social sector. As the government began withdrawing from social sectors, private agencies started taking its place charging higher user fee for their services. In this situation, the Dalits and tribals not only lost financial support from the government but were also forced to pay high user fees which they could not afford. Thus their education and health needs are really in jeopardy. The study will explore the effect of government withdrawal from social sectors on the tribals in Kerala.

In the light of globalisation, the state government made a major shift in educational policy when it privatised professional education, especially engineering and medicine. These measures have adversely affected SCs/STs as they do not get reservation and financial subsidy from these institutions. The government seems to be decreasing its investments in government hospitals and Public Health Centres (PHCs) also, which are mostly used by weaker sections like SCs/STs. The PDS in Kerala, which was the best in India, is badly affected by this shift in the policy of the Central Government. The information technology, which came very much as part of globalisation through advanced audio-visual media and communication, has reached every nook and corner of the state and has negatively affected the culture and lifestyle of the people, particularly of Adivasis. The present study will consider globalisation with respect to liberalisation, privatisation and withdrawal of government from social sectors, and their effect on the socioeconomic and cultural life of the tribals in Kerala.

Methods and Process of Data Collection

Both primary and secondary data have been effectively used in this study. Secondary data were collected from government and non-government organisations in the form of records, reports, books, journals and newspaper reports. For collecting primary data three methods were used, namely, a survey with schedule, case studies of three tribal villages in three districts, and unstructured personal interviews with a variety of people. Survey was the main source of data collection in this study. Eight hundred (800) tribal households, which formed about 1 per cent of total tribal households in Kerala, were selected from the three districts of Wayanad, Idukki and Palakkad according to the proportion of population of each district. The reasons for selecting these three districts for the present study are that they are the main districts for tribal inhabitants in Kerala and that they cover the major tribal communities of the state. Four hundred (400) respondents were selected from Wayanad and two hundred (200) each from Idukki and Palakkad.

For selecting the sample households a multistage stratified random sampling was used. The criteria of selection were taluk and panchayat representation and various tribal communities. Accordingly, in Wayanad which has the highest concentration of tribals in the state, all the three taluks of Mananthavady, Vythiri, and Sultan Bathery in the district were selected, and in each taluk as many panchayats as possible were covered. Six major tribal communities, namely Kurichyar, Mulluvakurummer, Adiyar, Paniyar, Kattunaikkar and Urali were included in the survey. Attapady in Palakkad district, which has the highest concentration of tribals in the district and which is also the only 'Tribal Block' in Kerala, was selected for the study. All the three panchayats of Attappady viz. Sholayur, Agaly and Puthur were chosen and two main tribal communities, Mudugar and Irular, were included in the sample. In Idukki, on the other hand, two out of four taluks (Peermadu and Devikulam) were selected for survey, and five major tribal groups in the districts (Paliyar, Mannan, Urali, Ullader and Muthuvan) were chosen for the interview. Samples were distributed among as many tribal colonies as possible in each taluk. In Devikulam taluk of Idukki district, Muthuvans, the leading tribal community in the district, who are living in remote forest land, were included in the sample. In short, the 800 samples truly represent the tribals in the state. It was decided to give at least 10 per cent of representation for women in the sample, but the actual representation has 30 per cent.

Since there are many limitations to the survey method especially with the population of tribals, the study also used case study to complement the data collected through schedules. One typical village of tribals in each district was selected in consultation with tribal leaders and social activists for a detailed and in-depth study on the impact of globalisation in that village. The study covered major areas of economic sphere including land, labour and the sociopolitical, religious and cultural life of the village during the last ten years. A brief history of the village and its myths and folklore were gathered, and a map of the village too was prepared. The objective of the case study was to analyse the transformation which has taken place in the selected tribal villages during the last ten years as a result of globalisation. Two of the persons who did the study were tribals themselves and the third was a social activist who had long years of experience of working with tribals. By selecting three villages in three districts we got an emic view of the tribal life in all the three districts.

The third method of data collection used for this study was personal interviews with a cross-section of people connected with tribals. They consisted of leaders of tribals and tribal organisations, social activists who are involved in the work among tribals, government officials, and representatives of political parties. About twenty people selected from all three districts were interviewed based on an interview guide.

To get a direct experience of the field and tribal situation in Kerala, the co-ordinator of the study, together with his research assistant, conducted an extensive tour of the major tribal colonies of all the three districts. They visited tribal colonies which are in remote areas in the forest and in mountain slopes. These visits helped them to have a first hand knowledge of the situation of the tribals, which in turn facilitated the work of preparing the interview schedule and of sampling process of the respondents, and of gathering of all other background data needed for the research study.

Field investigators for data collection were selected with the help of social workers and tribal leaders of each district. For Wayanad district there were seven field investigators, most of whom had many years of experience of working with tribals. In Palakkad, all the six field investigators were tribals, of whom four were women. In Idukki district, there were eight field investigators of whom four were tribals and four were post-graduate students. All the field investigators were given a minimum of three days of training in data collection and briefing on each of the three districts, which equipped them with necessary skills and knowledge for data collection.

The schedule for data collection was prepared based on the experience gathered by the coordinator and the research assistant while visiting major tribal colonies in all the three districts, and on discussion with tribal leaders, social activists and experts in research studies. First a pre-test of the schedule was conducted and its result analysed, and later the schedule was finalised and printed in Malayalam, the language of the state. Experts in the field processed the survey data by means of computer.

2

Tribals in Kerala

According to 2001 census the population of Scheduled Tribes (STs) in India was 84.33 million, which was about 8.2 per cent of the total population. About half of this tribal population is concentrated in the three states of Madhya Pradesh, Bihar and Orissa. The north-eastern states like Nagaland and Meghalaya have predominantly tribal communities forming more than 80 per cent of the total population.

The Gonds of Madhya Pradesh, Maharashtra and Andhra Pradesh, Bhils of Rajasthan and Gujarat, and Santals of Bihar, Orissa and West Bengal are the numerically dominant tribal communities in India (Velappan, 1994). Tribals in South India are comparatively less than in the northern states.

Among the STs there are differences based on race, language and culture. There are three main racial groups in India: Proto-Australoids, which form the most dominant group, consist of Munda, Orion, Ho, Ghond, Gond, etc. Mangols reside in the sub-Himalayan belt, especially in the North-East. Negritos who are found in many parts of the country, include Kadar, Paniyar, Irular, etc. of Kerala. The tribal languages in India belong to all the major language families: the Austric, the Dravidian and the Tibeto-Chinese. About 90 per cent of the tribals in India are considered "Hindus" by the census, 6 per cent are "Christians" and 4 per cent "others" (Mathur, 1977).

The majority of tribals live on agriculture or agriculture-related labour while others have occupations like hunting, gathering of forest produce, pasturing, and government jobs. Compared to the tribals in the North, those in the South are economically poorer, more primitive and more secluded from the mainstream communities. However, many of them are gradually getting integrated into the mainstream culture.

People and Place

According to 2001 census there are 364,189 tribals in Kerala, who constitute 1.14 per cent of the whole population. They were earlier known in Travancore-Cochin state as 'Kattu Jathi' and in Malabar as 'Kattukurumman', both meaning people of the forest. Today, they are known as 'Girijanam' or 'Girivarggam', meaning people of the hills. But they are generally called 'Adivasis' in Kerala as in other parts of India. They are mostly settled on the Western Ghats and hills bordering Karnataka and Tamil Nadu.

Though a small percentage of the population of the state, the tribals are divided into different communities. The number of communities differs according to various official studies and census. According to Mathur, there are 48 tribal communities (Mathur, 1977: 4), while according to Velappan there are 53 communities (Velappan, 1994: 22). In the government schedule 41 tribal communities are included. Among them the numerically dominant groups are Pulayans, Paniyans, Adiyans, Marratis, Malayarayars, Kurumas, Kuruchians, and Irulas. Though there are tribals in almost all the districts of Kerala they are most significantly found in Wayanad, Idukki, Palakkad, and Kasargod districts. Among all the districts, Wayanad has the highest concentration of tribals, constituting 17.43 per cent of the total tribal population in the state (2001).

The tribals settled in the state are divided into seven regions taking into account their ethnic and sociocultural relations (Mathur, 1977).

Kasargod

The region comprises the two taluks of Kasargod and Hosdurg of former Kannur district. The Koragas and Maratis are the most

Table 2.1
Distribution of Scheduled Tribes in Kerala

S.No.	District	General			Scheduled Tribes			Scheduled Tribes
		Total	Male	Female	Total	Male	Female	% of Total Population
1.	Thiruvananthapuram	3,234,356	1,569,917	1,664,439	20,893	9,890	11,003	0.65
2.	Kollam	2,585,208	1,249,621	1,335,587	5,190	2,447	2,743	0.20
3.	Pathanamthitta	1,234,016	589,398	644,618	6,549	3,184	3,365	0.53
4.	Alappuzha	2,109,160	1,014,529	1,094,631	3,131	1,565	1,566	0.15
5.	Kottayam	1,953,646	964,926	988,720	18,340	8,972	9,368	0.94
6.	Idukki	1,129,221	566,682	562,539	50,973	25,510	25,463	4.51
7.	Ernakulam	3,105,798	1,38,397	1,567,401	10,046	5,079	4,967	0.32
8.	Thrissur	2,974,232	1,422,052	1,552,180	4,826	2,293	2,533	0.16
9.	Palakkad	2,617,482	1,266,985	1,350,497	39,665	19,990	19,675	1.52
10.	Malappuram	3,625,471	1,754,576	1,870,895	12,267	5,996	6,271	0.34
11.	Kozhikode	2,879,131	1,399,358	1,479,773	5,940	2,924	3,016	0.21
12.	Wayanad	780,619	391,273	389,346	136,062	67,394	68,668	17.43
13.	Kannur	2,408,956	1,152,817	1,256,139	19,969	9,793	10,176	0.83
14.	Kasargod	1,204,078	588,083	615,995	30,338	15,132	15,206	2.52

Source: Census 2001.

important communities living in this area. The former, who are engaged in basket-making, are one of the most backward tribal communities in Kerala.

Wayanad

This region consists of the whole of the present Wayanad and Kannur districts. It has the highest percentage of tribals in Kerala (28%). It is nearly 3,000 feet above sea level. The communities which live in this region are Paniyans, Kurichians, Mullukurumans, Urali Kurumans, Kattunayakans, Kaders, Adiyans, Pulayans and Kalanadis (Mathur, 1977). They were formerly engaged in shifting cultivation, gathering of forest products and hunting, but now most of them have become agricultural labourers under the settlers.

Attappady

Situated at an elevation between 1,200 to 3,000 feet the region forms part of Mannarkkad taluk of Palakkad district. It is one of the prominent forest regions in the state that includes the famous evergreen forest of Silent Valley. The three main tribal communities inhabiting this region are Irulas, Mudugars, and Kurmbas. Attappady is the only Tribal Development Block in the state. The tribal population here has considerably declined due to large-scale migration of non-tribal settlers.

Nilambur

Nilambur, which is known for its evergreen forest, forms part of Manjeri taluk of Malappuram district. The important tribal groups living in this region are Cholanaikkans, Aranadans, Allars, Paniyans and Kurumans. Cholanaikkans who still live in caves are the most primitive tribal community in Kerala; they are food gatherers and collectors of minor forest produce.

Parambikulam

The region forms part of Chittur taluk of Palakkad district. The most important tribals who inhabit this region are the Kadars of Cochin, whose number is small and whose occupation is food gathering and collection of forest produce.

Idukki

The four taluks of Idukki district—Peerumade, Devikulam, Udumbumchola, and Thodupuzha, make up this tribal region. The major tribal communities found in this region are Uralies, Muthuvans, Hill Pulayans, Mannans, Malaulladans, and Mala Arayans and Palliyans.

Thiruvananthapuram

This region comprises Nedumangad and Neyyattinkara taluks of Trivandrum district and some parts of Pathanamthitta district. Kannikar and Malavedars are the prominent tribal communities in this region. Many of them have now taken up settled cultivation.

Livelihood of the Tribals in Kerala

The traditional sources of livelihood for tribals were hunting, collection of forest produce, basket and mat-making and shifting cultivation. These sources are now fast disappearing as forest laws prohibit them from freely entering the forests for hunting or collecting forest produce, and since many forests are getting dwindled. Yet some tribal communities that have not developed agriculture, such as the Kadars, Malapandarams, Malas, Ulladars, Malamalassars, Kattunaikkans, Aranadans, Mannars and Uralies, collect forest products including seeds, honey, and medicinal plants, and barter or sell them to the non-tribals. Their expertise in felling and collection of timber, bamboo and in collecting seeds is made use of also by non-tribals. Hunting and fishing are still practised by Maladevadars, Kuruchiars, Malaulladars and Malapandarams. Tribal communities such as Koragas, Malavettuvans, Mannans and Mavilans still earn some income from making baskets and mats.

When their traditional occupations got stopped, most of the tribal communities turned to agriculture or occupations related to it. As in the case of tribals all over India, shifting cultivation was the normal way of cultivation for them in the beginning. Under this method of cultivation, after clearing a forest and setting fire to it they cultivate; after the harvest, the tribals move to another location for cultivation by the same method. The tribals had a very primitive way of cultivation as regards technology, seeds, instruments etc. Axe, knife, sharp nails, bow and arrow, spear, hook and line were some of the tools they used for all their occupations. Most of the tribals who have land today are engaged in settled agriculture, though their method of cultivation is not fully modernised. Adiyans, Ervalans, Irullars, Paniyans, Kuruchiars, Mavilans, Kannikars and Malaaryans are some of the groups who are engaged in agriculture. However, very few of them employ modern methods of farming like ploughing and the use of irrigation. Ragi, maize, tapioca, ginger, cardomom, pepper, pulses and coffee are some of the crops cultivated by tribals.

In olden times some of the tribals in Wayanad district were bought and sold as slaves for paddy cultivation (Panoor, 1993). Most of them were Paniyas who were brought from Karnataka and Tamil Nadu border by 'Jenmis', the landlords. The tribal slaves were auctioned, sold and bought for Rs 10 to 30 per person at the annual festival of Valliyurkavu temple in Wayanad. The contract was for one year to work under one landlord till the festival the following year. For some years the system continued. Later when plantations and estates were established they became labourers. When settlers came, they made the Adivasis labourers and even bonded labourers. They were highly exploited with long hours of work and meagre wages often given in kind in the form of paddy (Velappan, 1994; Kattakayam, 1983).

The staple food of most of the tribes in Kerala is rice. Maize, ragi, cereals, herbs, and roots are some of the other items of food. Almost all the tribes eat meat. Some tribals like Muthuvans, Urali-Kurumans and Paniyas eat crabs, prawns and snails. All the tribals drink coffee and tea. Many of the tribes use alcohol and know the art of brewing alcoholic drinks from rice, and tapping toddy from the palm tree. Practically all the tribal groups chew betel nut, pan and tobacco (Kattakkayam, 1983). The clothing pattern of most of the tribal groups has already been adapted to that of the mainstream population.

Sociopolitical Life of the Tribals in Kerala

Nuclear family is the common form of family among the tribals in Kerala. It could be father, mother, and their unmarried children, or husband, wife and their children and unmarried brothers and sisters. Joint-family system is rare among them. Till recently, there were no clear-cut rules about property ownership. Among the settled tribals, property was handed down from father to son. In some communities, however, matriarchal system is prevalent while in others it is a mixture of both matriarchal and patriarchal. Most of the tribals in Wayanad follow patriarchal system while many in Palakkad district follow the matriarchal system.

Social Structure

Normally, there is a headman for each tribal settlement with 15–20 houses. Different names such as 'Moopan', 'Kanikaran', 'Ponamban', 'Melvaka' and 'Sthani' are prevalent for the headman among different communities. The headman is in charge of the social needs of the community, apart from providing rituals and medicine. He presides over the council of elders to make decisions with regard to the social life of the tribals. People are supposed to obey the orders and decisions of the leader and to respect him. They are also supposed to get his permission for marriage and funeral rite. In return for the services of the headman, who is the leader of the settlement, adults from the village give free labour for his cultivation and look after his other needs. In time of famine the grain from the store of the headman is distributed among the people. In all the tribal groups except among Kuruchias, leadership is hereditary. Among the Mannans of Idukki there is a king (Rajamannans). A silver stick or a sword or a knife is used by the leader of a few adivasi communities as a symbol of his authority. Each of the tribal communities is divided into clans and the members of a clan are considered to be brothers and sisters. Thus inter-marriage is prohibited among them. The tribal social structure is based on blood relationship and marriage, but this social structure is fast changing due to external influence.

The Adivasi huts or houses are made of bamboos and thatched with grass. The floor is at the level of the ground. The walls of the house are built with split bamboo pieces or clay. Instead of windows there are holes in the wall. The name of the hut differs from community to community, and are called Chala, Chitara, Palli, Kudi, Pire etc. In olden times houses were built on the treetop to protect the tribals from wild animals. However, as a result of contact with mainstream population a lot of changes are taking place in the social structure and customs of the tribals in Kerala.

Marriage Customs

'Stealing' or 'capturing the bride' was one type of marriage among many tribal communities. The girl was forcefully carried away by the bridegroom or his relatives and later the marriage would be celebrated by both the parties. This custom is almost gone today, but its remnant is existing in certain tribes like the Muthuvans. The bride with her friends hides in a forest. The relatives of the bridegroom go in search of her and take her to the bridegroom. On the way back her girl friends sing a lot of romantic songs in a group.

Instead of dowry, a system of giving money to the girl's father by the bridegroom's father existed among most tribal communities. Among some tribals including Malavedars, Malankuruvars, Thandapulayars, Irulars, Kurumbars etc., this custom is still prevalent. Among a few tribal groups this kind of exchange of money has to be repeated every year. The amount given is called 'Kanapanam' or 'Piripanam' in certain communities. If there is a divorce, this money has to be returned to the donor. There is also a custom existing even today among the Mannans, Malayars, Uralies, Paniyars, Kurumbars and others, of giving one's work as free service to the father of the bride. The bridegroom gives his labour for a period of time to the father before marriage. Among Uralies of Idukki district is a prevalent practice even today of mutually exchanging sisters for marriage. If a man has more than one sister he can get more than one wife, and if he has not got a sister he will not get a wife and will be forced to remain a bachelor. The custom of marrying one's niece (Marumakkathayam) is also prevalent among some Adivasi communities. Malayalars, a small Adivasi community, marry among blood relations only. The right of a widow to marry the brother of her husband, and of a widower to marry the sister of his wife is prevalent among most tribal communities.

Tying 'thali' and presenting new clothes are common practices among tribals. Among 'Karavazhi pulayars', the practice of bridegroom and bride sitting on a mat facing and feeding each other with rice is the main marriage ritual. Touching each other's head a few times and then mutually feeding with rice is a custom among Kanikars. Pulayars have their marriage ceremony early in the morning. They make the couple stand on a grinder, hold each other's hands and exchange betel leaves. But many of these marriage customs are disappearing from the life of tribals. Segregation of people at certain times is common among many Adivasi communities—girls attaining puberty and women during menstrual period and delivery time were kept in separate houses. Adult girls and boys had to stay separately in a special common building called 'Chavadikal'. This was practised mainly among the Muthuvans. At such times others are not permitted to have contact with them.

Status of Tribal Women

"In most of the tribal communities in Kerala and Wayanad in particular, the women enjoy equal status with their menfolk. The women are the corner stones of the social structure of tribal societies of Wayanad" (Mathur, 1977: 154). When shifting cultivation was prevalent, women had an important role in farming besides her role in keeping the house, feeding and raising the family, and maintaining social relations. When cash economy was introduced, she became the controller of cash and the household.

Women in tribal society in Kerala have certain economic and social equality and position. They are equal partners in family and conjugal life although they do not enjoy pre-marital freedom. There are both patrilineal and matrilineal societies among the tribals. Among some tribes the former, and among others, the latter system is practiced. But supreme domination of matriarchy is not practiced among tribals in Kerala (Mathur, 1977: 154–55). Divorce is practised among all tribal communities, and widow remarriage is also prevalent.

Though tribal women have an important position in society, they are debarred from exercising power over land. Neither do they hold any position of authority. No woman can be a chieftain. Ownership of property is vested with males, though in a matrilineal society males get a share. Male children are preferred by tribal parents. Women do not perform any rituals or ceremonies, nor are they allowed to practice magic or sorcery. Therefore, though tribal women enjoy certain status and freedom with regard to marriage and family as compared to their counterparts in other societies in Kerala, in economic and sociopolitical spheres they do not have much functional role. Today they are losing even the limited roles they had in olden times. Even tribal women in matrilineal societies do not enjoy a superior position than those among patrilineal societies. The status of tribal women can be improved through progressive economic and educational emancipation (Mathur, 1977).

Cultural Life of the Tribals in Kerala

Religion and Beliefs

Animism, totemism and polytheism are various forms of religious practices prevalent among tribals of Kerala. But Hindu religion and its practices are increasingly influencing them. Worship of ancestors is very common among them. They believe in the existence of soul and life after death and they treat the supernatural with fear. They also have fear of death and so they offer sacrifices and offerings to propitiate evil forces. Alongside they resort to magic and divination so that the gods could intervene in their life to protect them from evil. Some tribals resort to magic to cure illness, though this practice is fast disappearing. Sastha, Kali, Siva, Murugan, Vishnu and Ayyappan, who are Hindu gods, are worshipped widely among the tribals, in place of nature deities like 'malavazhis'. Their practice of animism is expressed in worship of inanimate objects. So trees, rocks and caves are believed to have supernatural powers and are worshipped even today by many tribals. Worship of the sun is practiced among Uralies, Muthuvans and Koragas. Some tribals like Kurumbas, Irulas and Paniyans perform live sacrifice, and offerings are eaten after the ceremony. Among Kanikars, Palliyans and Kuruvans, many have been converted to Christianity (Velappan, 1994; Kattakkyaam, 1983).

There are priests and sorcerers to perform religious rites. Among a few tribals they are called "Palthikal". Totemism, by which a clan traced its origin to some hill, animal or a tree and by which the members of the clan considered themselves blood-related, was much prevalent in olden times but it is slowly disappearing now (Velappan, 1994).

Culture and Language

The art of tribals is an expression of their close relationship with nature. Music and dance are intermingled in their cultural forms. Malayarayars have songs called 'Kelapattukal' which they sing while preparing the field for cultivation and harvesting and also for rocking the children. They also have a group dance called 'Kambukali' and single dance called 'Ulakakali'. Mannans have a musical dance drama called "Koothu". Among Uralikurummers there is a religious practice called 'Daivam kanal' which is used to find solutions to life problems like illness and calamities. Adiyans have a mixture of art, science and religion in their practice called 'Gadhikam Song', which is used to cure illness. Irulars express their acting skill in 'Karadiyattam' by imitating the movement of tigers. 'Pallyarkali', 'Vedarkali', 'Kadarkali' and 'Onakali' are some of the many cultural forms prevalent among tribal communities in Kerala. Thudi, Davile, Kozhale, Maram and Karivi are some of the well-known musical instruments of Adivasis.

All the tribal communities have their own languages, though they do not have distinct identities. The languages of Muthuvans and Mannans of Idukki are said to have distinct identities, according to some scholars. Many tribal languages are believed to be variations of Malayalam and 75 per cent of the language of Paniyas in Wayanad forms part of Malayalam. However, most of the communities have a mixture of Malayalam, Tamil and Kannada (Velappan, 1994).

Land Alienation of Tribals in Kerala

The police firing on the tribals at Muthanga in Wayanad district of Kerala in February 2003 leading to the death of an Adivasi and a policeman and hundreds of Adivasis including women and children getting injured was very much highlighted at the national level. The encroachment of land by Adivasis at Muthanga and in different parts of Kerala were expressions of anger and frustration of Adivasis over the apathy of the government towards the problem of their land and life. The desperate acts of the most marginalised community can be understood if the process and methods of land alienation of tribals in Kerala are analysed.

Early Situation of Tribal Land in Kerala

The situations of tribals were different in the three erstwhile states of Travancore, Cochin and Malabar, which make up the present-day Kerala. In Malabar, the northern part of Kerala which was under the Madras Presidency, the tribals who were living in the forest around the present Wayanad district bordering the areas of Karnataka and Tamil Nadu, were made slaves by the traditional landlords (Jenmis) for their paddy cultivation. "Historically, Paniyans and Adiyans who constitute 27 per cent of total tribal population in the state, were agrestic slaves and had been subjected to the highest degree of inhuman treatment in the hands of the traditional 'Jenmis' " (Kunhaman, 1989: 21). When plantations started developing in Wayanad the new settlers from central Kerala made them labourers, and later bonded labourers and coolie workers. Attappady, the second largest tribal concentration in Kerala in Palakkad district, had a slightly different story. When the immigrants from Travancore, Cochin and Tamil Nadu migrated to this area in the 1950s dispossessing the tribals of their land, they withdrew to the interior areas of forests. In the princely state of Cochin the tribal population which was small, got settled with agriculture by the end of the 19th century, though shifting cultivation was practiced among a few tribal groups. The princely state of Travancore gave ownership rights to the Adivasis in the forest by the end of the same century with legal protection of the land from non-tribals, various encouragements for cultivation and permission to use forest for their livelihood. Except for a few non-advanced tribals others availed themselves of the helps and facilities. Based on these geographical, political and historical differences there were two types of tribals in the reorganised Kerala state—the landless and the landed. According to the Socioeconomic Survey of Tribals in Kerala (Government of Kerala, 1979), 30 per cent of the Adivasis in Kerala are landless. But in Wayanad district it is about 61 per cent. According to a study made in 1975, during the decade 1966–76, 44 per cent of the total alienated land was in Palakkad. In short, most of the tribals in Kerala had land in the beginning, but gradually many of them lost their land due to various factors like the land policy of the British, immigration, land reforms, developmental projects and lack of legal protection for the tribal land.

Land Policy of the British

The tribal communities everywhere were egalitarian with common ownership of land and they cultivated the land only for what was needed for their sustenance. But the British introduced the "settlement" of land based on private ownership recognised through legal deeds, records and complicated measurement processes. They implemented these laws in Malabar which formed part of Madras Presidency. The new regulations were totally alien to the tribals who were not able to understand and assimilate the new system with its elaborate legal process and ownership titles. Therefore, they did not bother to get ownership deeds for their land. Exploiting this situation, the traditional landlords and later the settlers dispossessed the Adivasis of their land in Malabar area as had happened in most parts of India. After World War II, the British and later the Indian Government encouraged agriculture and farmers. In 1948, the Madras Presidency brought out a scheme for ex-servicemen, by which it distributed land with title deeds in Wayanad to ex-servicemen and some landless people including some tribals. But the scheme was generally detrimental to the tribal interest. Thus the British land policy adversely affected the Adivasis.

Entry of the Settlers

The encouragement from the government, in addition to the population increase and the subsequent increase in unemployment, motivated many Christians, Hindus and Muslims from Travancore and Cochin to migrate to Malabar, Palakkad and different parts of the Western Ghats in the 1950s. As there was no law in Kerala to protect tribal land, the settlers easily got and bought the tribal land using devious methods to cheat the simple and illiterate Adivasis.

The settlers also exploited the indebtedness of the poor tribals by often operating provision shops and liquor shops in the tribal areas. Since the Adivasis were not sure of the exact prices of things and were illiterate, they could easily be cheated. The traders manipulated the accounts of the Adivasis and calculated interest upon interest, and thus their debt swelled to a point of their not being not able to pay back. In such a situation they would lease out their land and when they were not able to pay back the debt, they would surrender their land. During the emergency, the government waived off the debt of an Adivasi belonging to Kanikkar group in Trivandrum district and gave him back three acres of arecanut plantation, which was mortgaged to a person. After the emergency period the creditor approached him for his money. Though the officials had instructed him not to bother about the old loan, the Adivasi gave back the land on the ground that he had to honour the contract. Through these kinds of fraudulent transactions, people exploited the truthfulness and ignorance of the Adivasis and thus took away their land. It is said that 28 per cent of land was alienated in Wayanad due to indebtedness.

Fraudulent transactions through manipulated records also often forced the Adivasis to surrender their land. If there was any dispute over land the police in connivance with the revenue officials would threaten the Adivasis and take the side of the settlers. The Adivasis would be helpless when the court asked for documents and evidence. Most of the land deals in Idukki district in the 1960s were said to be of this type. A Paniya woman named Chunda Panichi borrowed Rs 100 from a settler and in return she gave him four acres of land on lease. After three years, she asked him to return the land, which he refused. The relatives of Chunda tried to occupy the land by force. But the settler got an injunction from the court and prevented them from entering the land. He himself set fire to a hut he had constructed and Chunda and her relatives were arrested on this charge. In the long legal battle that followed, the tribal woman lost the case due to lack of evidence for the boundaries of her land (Mathur, 1977). According to a study, 1.1 per cent of land alienation was by means of force and cheating.

According to the Socioeconomic Survey of Tribal Communities in Kerala (Government of Kerala, 1979) the rate of land alienation was at its highest during the 1950s in the district of Malabar, which was also the peak period of immigration into the tribal areas. During the decade ending 1976, 3,546 tribal families lost almost 9,859 acres of land. A study by the Kerala Agricultural University made in 1992 shows that two-thirds of tribals under study in Wayand district lost their land due to the immigration by non-tribals. The tribal population also decreased drastically after the non-tribals started occupying Adivasi areas. For example, according to Mathur (1996), in Attappady in Palakkad district the tribal population was about 90 per cent in 1951. It came down to 63 per cent in 1961 and to 43 per cent in 1971. While the tribals increased by about 45 per cent over a decade, the non-tribals increased by 150 per cent. Just as the Blacks in Africa were enslaved and their countries were conquered, and the Red-Indians in America were annihilated and their land was captured, in a similar process the tribals in Kerala were dispossessed of their land (Panoor, 1990).

Those tribals who retained their land as in Palakkad district were pushed back by the immigrants to interior areas of forests, where often the land was infertile and rocky and sloppy. In other words, the fertile land of the tribals was encroached upon by the non-tribal plainsmen (Kunhamen, 1989).

Land Reform Measures

It is a paradox that the Adivasis lost their land due to progressive land reform laws of Kerala, but it did happen. The tribals used to lease out their land for cultivation to the rich immigrants who were considered tenants. According to the land reform law, the tenants would be entitled to get the land after a certain period of time and after paying nominal compensation in many instalments. Making use of this law, many rich settlers got the tribal land and the Adivasis did not get even the prescribed compensation due to the complicated process.

The land reform laws, which are supposed to benefit the poorest and most marginalised groups in society like tribals have taken away even the little land they had, and impoverished them further. The people who have to be protected by the law have become the victims of the same law! The utter disregard of the ruling class and the governments of Kerala for the most marginalised people, is a clear example of how a group which does not have political power and influence is ignored and marginalised by them.

Developmental Projects of the Government

As had happened all over India, many tribals lost their land in Kerala on account of developmental projects like dams and forestry operations. Many tribals lost their land because of Idukki, Chimmini and Karapusha dams, the major hydroelectric and irrigation projects in Kerala. Since the Adivasis did not possess any valid documents of their land, they were deprived of their rightful compensation too. Even when they got it, a good percentage of it was swallowed up by the unscrupulous middlemen. The Central Forest Acts and state forest laws also affected the tribals in Kerala as they did elsewhere in India. By setting aside forests as reserved forest and wildlife sanctuary like Muthanga and leasing out forests to big factories to plant and cut trees like eucalyptus, tribals were dispossessed of their forest land. Worse still, they were denied access to the forest produce, including food, fuel and fodder, which were part of life-support for their meagre living. The children of the forest were in a sense driven out of their habitat.

Lack of Laws to Protect Tribal Land

Schedule V of Article 244 of the Constitution directs the state to ensure by suitable legislation, total prohibition of transfer of tribal land to non-tribals. The Dhebar Commission in 1960 also recommended that all tribal land alienated since 1950 should be returned to the tribals. But the Government of Kerala miserably failed to pass the necessary laws to protect tribal land. It passed a legislation in 1975 only after states like Andhra Pradesh had done so, that too under the pressure of the emergency. But the rules for operationalising the law that was called Kerala Scheduled Tribes Restriction on Transfer of Lands and Restoration of Alienated Lands Act came only after a decade, in 1986. According to the Act, land transactions of Adivasis done after 1960 were held invalid and had to be returned. By that time, immigration to the tribal land and to the Western Ghats was almost complete. Later an amendment was made, by which the land alienated only after 1987 was to be returned, but this also was not implemented.

Due to intervention by and pressure from the High Court, the government enacted another law in 1996, which however did not get the President's assent. In 1999, the government brought out yet another law called 'Kerala Restriction on Transfer and Restoration of Lands to Scheduled Tribes Bill', according to which land in excess of two hectares would be restored while alternate land would be provided for the rest in lieu of alienated land. But the government failed to implement even this innocuous and ineffective law. Thus, in spite of long legal battles, the tribals have not got back their alienated land nor have they got alternate land. The greatest injustice done to the Adivasis by the government is that it did not pass a law to protect tribal land as required by the Constitution in proper time, and that it did not implement even the diluted laws enacted later. Since both the United Democratic Front and the Left Democratic Front alternately ruled the state during this long period of history, both are equally responsible for the neglect of tribals in Kerala. The interest of the land-owning class was more important for the two governments than that of the poor tribals.

Constitutional Safeguards and Welfare Measures for the Tribals in Kerala

It is the duty of the government to promote the welfare of weaker sections of its people especially the SC/ST. It should protect them from injustice and all types of exploitation (Const. 4/46). Schedule 341, 342 of the Constitution authorise the President of India to declare a certain caste or a tribe as a Scheduled Caste or Tribe in each state from time to time.

According to the Constitution the responsibility of protecting the needs of the tribals is entrusted to the President of India, the Parliament, the Governors and the Assemblies in each state. A Director General is in charge of weaker sections at the national level with regional level directors. The SC/ST Minister, together with the Chief Minister, is supposed to implement these programmes for the Governor in each state. There is to be a Tribal Advisory Council and Tribal Research Institute in each state. In short, the Constitution makes various provisions to protect the interests of the SCs/STs, and gives the mechanism and structures to implement them (Velappan, 1994). The

Constitution also provides reservation of seats for tribals in Parliament and State Assemblies, in Union and State Government jobs and in educational institutions run by the government. The government sets apart 10 per cent of all developmental plan budget for the welfare programmes of SC/ST population.

The Kerala government created a Department of Tribal Welfare and also a Tribal Research and Training Centre under a Director. All the programmes of tribals are channeled through this department. The Directorate has five regional offices at Manathavady, Nilambur, Mannarkat, Thodupuzha and Punalur under a Tribal Department Officer.

Initially, Five-Year Plans did not have special plan outlay for SCs/STs but from the Fifth Plan, a 'Special Component Plan' was fixed as a percentage of the total plan outlay of the state in proportion to its SC/ST population. Though the idea was good, often the fund earmarked was lower than the proportion of the population, the schemes were not relevant to the target group and above all, there was leakage of funds. So, from 1983 onwards, the Kerala government transferred the Special Component Plan to the district level working groups for SC/ST development with District Collector as Chairman and District Planning Officer as Convenor.

Together with Special Component Plan a 'Tribal Sub-Plan' was constituted during the Fifth Plan by Kerala to "promote the socioeconomic conditions of the Scheduled Tribes and free them from exploitation" (*Economic Review*, 2002: 311). To achieve this objective, Integrated Tribal Development Projects (ITDPs), with focus on socio-economic development of tribal communities, were started. Special projects like Suganthagiri Cardamom Project and Attappady Co-operative Farming Society were part of this project. Several ITDPs were initiated in the state between 1975 and 1989. However, the Tribal Sub-Plan was never fully operationalised in the state since in an administrative area non-tribals constituted a majority of the population. Therefore, from 1983 onwards it was decentralised at the district level. In 1997, a major portion of Tribal Sub-Plan and Special Component Plan was devolved to the local self-government.

Without people's participation, however, the Special Component Plan and Sub-Plan tended to be bureaucratic. This anomaly was to be corrected by implementing the whole plan through local self-governments started in 1997 with the Ninth Five-Year Plan, as part of People's Plan Campaign in Kerala. With this idea about 65–70 per cent of funds from Special Component Plan and Tribal Sub-Plan were allotted to local self-governments. District-level committees, consisting of officials and social activists, were formed for the planning, implementation and monitoring of projects at district level, in place of the existing district level working groups. Separate task forces were constituted in all local self-governments for preparation of projects for tribals. Instead of Grama Sabhas, 'Oorukootams' (traditional tribal panchayats) were to identify projects and their beneficiaries and social activists from tribal areas were to assist this process of people's participation. Housing, drinking water, sanitation and education were priority areas in the planning. A total of Rs 1,149 crores was earmarked to local self-governments for tribals during the first five annual plans of the Ninth Five-Year Plan.

Table 2.2

Plan Grant to Local Self-Governments for Special Component Plan and Tribal Sub-Plan in Kerala (1997–98 to 2001–2002)

Annual Plans	*Plan Grant to Local Self-Governments (Rs Crore)*		
	Special Component Plan	*Tribal Sub-Plan*	*Total*
1	*2*	*3*	*4*
1997–98	194	39	233
1998–99	195	39	234
1999–2000	200	40	240
2000–2001	217	43	260
2001–02	182	0	182
Total	988	161	1149

Source: Economic Review, 2002, GOK, 2003, p. 312.

Some of the schemes and programmes being implemented by the state government for tribals are given below. The schemes implemented are classified into five categories: (1) Economic Development, (2) Education, (3) Social Development, (4) Reservations, and (5) Miscellaneous Concessions.

Economic Development

The following programmes are under economic development: land assignment, concessional lease of government lands, special land concessions to Kanikkars of Neyyattinkara taluk, land acquisition for house sites to individual applicants, house construction scheme, grants for the reclamation of lands and purchase of agricultural implements, grants to institutions and organisations, formation of co-operative societies, industrial training, legal aid, and subsidy to technically trained persons.

Educational Schemes

Educational schemes cover fee concessions, fees for prematriculation courses, lumpsum grant and stipend for prematriculation courses, post-matriculation grants, educational concessions for students staying outside the state of Kerala, miscellaneous items of educational help such as reservation of seats in educational institutions, relaxation in minimum marks for admission, age relaxation, etc., welfare hostels, vocational study, welfare schools and tribal schools, adult education, night schools, and Government of India scholarships.

Social Development Schemes

These involve eradication of untouchability, provision of common buildings, libraries and reading-rooms. Public health programmes consisting of: ayurvedic, allopathic and homeo dispensaries, hospitals and primary health centres, mobile medical units, provision of wells, street-lighting, approach roads, latrines, and cremation grounds (Rohini, mimeo, 1994: 127–29).

Employment Schemes

These consist of financial assistance to technically trained tribals to start self-employment, financial help for agricultural operations and implements, conversion of existing training centres into production-cum-training centres, practical training in forest related occupations such as sawing and wood works, industrial training in trades like carpentry and weaving. There are 23 such training centres in Kerala, which provide vocational training with monthly stipend. Adult-education with a scheme for conducting study tours and excursions for primitive tribals is also part of this scheme.

Other programmes earmarked for the tribals are: housing scheme by which the government gives grant to tribal households for construction and improvement of houses, financial assistance for various needs of tribals like marriages, Mahila Samajams (Government of Kerala, 1998), development institutions like Kerala Institute for Research, Training and Development Studies which is an institute to conduct research studies on SCs/STs in Kerala, and Kerala State Development Corporation for SCs/STs providing about 60 types of schemes for asset creation and employment generation for tribals (Government of Kerala, 2003: 316–17).

Present Situation of Tribals in Kerala

In spite of many constitutional provisions, legal benefits and welfare measures accorded to the tribals in India as mentioned above, they are still the most backward community in all respects throughout India, particularly in Kerala. These constitutional and legal rights except reservation are not enforced due to lack of political will. Most of the welfare and developmental measures provided through Special Component Plan and Tribal Sub-Plan have not benefited the tribals substantially as they were not implemented properly. The huge allocation of money is either not spent or diverted to undeserving hands. As a result, the situation of the tribals in Kerala basically remains the same or has worsened. They are facing myriads of problems in all spheres of life like land alienation, loss of forest, poverty, problems of health, education and housing, and loss of cultural life. This section explains the present socioeconomic situation of tribals in Kerala.

Land Alienation and Economic Backwardness

Land alienation has already been explained in an earlier section. Adivasis' life is closely linked with land and forest. Land is considered to be the most important resource in almost all tribal areas (Negi, 1986: 20) while forest provided food, fodder and raw materials to them and thus was a source of supplementary income and life support. But the "tribal who formerly regarded himself as 'lord' of the forest was, through a deliberate process, turned into a subject and placed under the forest department" (Roy Berman, quoted in Budhadev Chaudhuri, 1982: 79). The forest department put many restrictions which prevented the tribals from accessing the privileges and resources of the forest. The loss of land and forest has reduced them to the status of casual wage labour, and they have been constrained to buy most of their requirements from the market. Thus, the traditional self-reliant, non-monetised tribal economy got gradually transformed into a 'dependent' and monetised economy which became highly vulnerable to the external economic and social environment. This had an impact on the perceptions and aspirations of the new generation of tribals. In contrast to the self-reliant and contented life of the earlier generations, the present generation aspires for better living conditions, housing and enhanced social status (Mohandas, 1992: 143).

In other words, the Adivasi economy, which was non-commercialised became commercialised, so that, unlike in earlier times, they had to depend on market for everything they needed. This means they needed income in the form of money to meet their daily needs in life. The only source of income was employment as labourers for wages. Unfortunately work was often not available and naturally they did not have money and income to purchase even essential commodities. The result was poverty, indebtedness and even starvation deaths.

Land alienation is the main problem for most tribals in Kerala. At the same time, a sizeable section of tribals has land. But today they are not able to make a living out of cultivation of land. Some tribals follow traditional subsistent farming, some are engaged in commercial farming mainly with cash crops, while some are engaged in farming with a combination of subsistent and commercial farming. Subsistent farming here means cultivation for family consumption without having surplus for market. Commercial farming, on the other hand, is cultivation for market. Whatever be the type of farming, certain features are common to all tribal agriculture. They are: primitive methods and tools of cultivation, reluctance to adopt modern methods of agriculture like use of high yielding seeds and use of manure whether natural or chemical, single-crop cultivation, lack of irrigation facilities, and low productivity (Negi, 1986). Because of primitive methods of cultivation, land is not a sure source of livelihood for tribals, especially since the price of most agricultural crops is very low. Therefore, along with the effort of restoring land to the tribals, it is important that they are helped to solve the above deficiencies in the mode of their cultivation.

Poor Standard of Living

The economic level of tribals in Kerala is very low. With land alienation, agriculture is not able to provide adequate income for a living. Even those who have farms need to supplement it with their coolie work, and more than half of them are agricultural labourers. The percentage of those in the organised sector is very low. Due to low earning and lack of assets the incidence of poverty is relatively high among them (*Economic Review*, 2000).

When employment opportunities were drastically reduced the tribals were forced to take loans at exorbitant rate of interest even for their basic needs. Thus indebtedness became another major problem for the tribals. "Indebtedness and land alienation are the two main problems confronting the tribes of Kerala" (Kattakayam, 1983: 47).

Table 2.3

SC/ST Employees in Government Service in Kerala

Category	*Total*	*SC*	*ST*
Gazetted	27,839	2,904	406
Non-Gazetted (Excluding Last Grade)	274,901	26,692	2,929
Last Grade	43,666	5,918	671
Total	346,406	35,514	4,006

Source: Employment Cell, Government Secretariat, Thiruvananthapuram (*Economic Review*: 2002).

According to the table, only 4,006 tribals were there in government service in Kerala, which is very low for more than 1 per cent of population. On the other hand, Scheduled Castes (SCs) have 35,514 government employees. Thus tribals are far behind Dalits in employment in government service.

Table 2.4

SC/ST Students at School Level in Kerala

Section	*Total*	*Scheduled Caste*	*Percentage Total*	*Scheduled Tribes*	*Percentage Total*
Lower Primary Section	1,629,837	208,774	12.81	27,784	1.70
Upper Primary Section	1,381,358	163,916	11.87	18,231	1.32
High School Section	1,416,612	160,502	11.33	13,060	0.92
Total	4,427,807	533,192	12.04	59,075	3.94

Source: Directorate of Public Instruction (*Economic Review*: 2002).

The table shows that the proportion of ST students in schools is only 3 per cent. Drop-out rate in classes I-VIII is 31 per cent compared to 0.90 per cent in Kerala overall. This is an indication of the low level of education among tribal children.

Table 2.5
SC/ST Students in Arts and Science Colleges in Kerala

Course	*Total Strength*	*Scheduled Castes*	*Percentage to Total*	*Scheduled Tribes*	*Percentage to Total*
Degree	145,979	13,547	9.28	999	0.68
Post-Graduation	14,775	1,530	10.35	135	0.91
Total	160,754	15,077	9.38	1,134	1.59

Source: Directorate of Collegiate Education (*Economic Review*: 2002).

The table shows that tribal children studying in degree and post-graduation are 1,134, which is a mere 2 per cent of the total number of students in degree colleges in Kerala.

Table 2.6
SC/ST Students in Technical Institutions in Kerala

Institutions	*Total*	*Scheduled Castes*	*Scheduled Tribes*
Engineering Colleges	8,986	718	180
Polytechnics	18,600	1,488	186
Technical High Schools	3,510	280	40
Total	31,096	2,486	406

Source: Directorate of Technical Education (*Economic Review*: 2002).

The table shows that total number of tribal students in technical education including engineering, is only 406, which is abysmally low in a highly literate state. Lack of education is a major stumbling block for tribals to attain higher standard of life. Many factors stand in the way of improvement in education, including expenses involved in education, heavy drop-out rate, medium of instruction, and lack of employment even for educated tribals.

Lack of Medical Facilities and Housing

Lack of good drinking water, inadequate protection from natural calamities and poor communication facilities are some of the problems which make the tribals susceptible to diseases. They resort to tribal medicines and witchcraft instead of adopting modern medicine, though increasingly they are using them. The Ayurvedic dispensaries, public health centres and hospitals are not adequate since they do not have medicines and medical facilities. Birth-rate among tribals is very low, though the family planning programmes have not penetrated much into the community. They resort to tribal methods of abortion and birth control (Kattakayam, 1983).

According to the assessment of the government, "housing is the most seriously felt basic need" (*Economic Review*, 2000). Government grant is available for tribals for housing and many tribals make use of this facility. Thus in many colonies they have tiled or pucca houses. But in some districts where tribals are not aware of their rights and benefits, they find the procedure cumbersome. Non-tribals exploit their ignorance and take a sizeable portion as commission for the help rendered to get the money sanctioned by the government. Besides, the contractors entrusted with the construction of the house do the work poorly taking a huge portion as profit.

Loss of Tribal Culture and Social Structure

Since many tribals in Kerala are uprooted from land and traditional support systems, they are also uprooted from their culture and lifestyle. The social organisation of tribals is gradually getting disintegrated with the erosion of coherence and unity of tribal communities. The influence and authority of Moopan, the traditional leader, in tribal socioreligious life has declined. This means that the traditional leadership has lost its hold on the community. Joint management of family property based on joint family system has virtually disappeared partly due to the influence of values of individualism and partly due to private property of the settlers.

When their socioeconomic base structure was destroyed tribals increasingly fell victim to alcoholism. Non-tribals used this weapon to get their land and their services for illegal felling of forest trees and even for brewing of illicit liquor. This has ruined their family life and remains a block to their socioeconomic emancipation and progress.

Organisational Growth of Tribals in Kerala

As explained above, the tribals in Kerala were facing myriads of problems. They lost their land and access to forest, which were their life-support. They had poor standard of living, education and health facilities. They were almost uprooted from their culture and social life. It was in this background that they started getting organised either by themselves or with the help of others.

One of the earliest tribal organisations in Wayanad district was Wayanad Adivasi Swayam Sevak Sangham (WASSS), which was founded in 1963 and registered in 1969 with mostly tribal members. It adopted dharnas, picketing and satyagrahas to achieve their demands like exemption of stamp duty for tribal litigants and restoration of alienated tribal land. This functioned till 1972. In 1968 the Karshaka Thozhilali Union (Agricultural Labourers' Union) was formed by CPI(M) to fight the bonded labour system. It conducted dharnas and satyagrahas to meet its demands. Later the leadership passed on to the Naxalites who, among other acts of violence, murdered a Brahmin landlord. The leaders were later shot dead by the police and many tribal members were convicted.

The Wayanad Adivasi Sangham, a splinter group of WASSS, was formed in 1969 with the support of Jan Sangh. Over 90 per cent of its members were Kurichiyas. Another splinter organisation was founded in 1975 with the name Kerala Girivarga Sangham, by a CPI(M) tribal ex-MLA. Its main objective was to terrorise the non-tribal settlers. With the Emergency in 1975, the organisation became defunct.

The Kerala Adivasi Samajam was formed by the Indian National Congress in 1973. The majority of its members were Mullukurumas. The Samajam claimed that the Central Acts prohibiting bonded labour and state laws preventing alienation of land and restoration of alienated tribal land, were adopted due to their effort. In addition to these organisations, there were other community-based tribal organisations that were formed between 1970 and 1992, independent of political parties, like Kurumma Samudaya Samrakshana Samithi and Kerala Paniya Samajam. Most of these organisations were confined to different tribal communities. They were also controlled mostly by outsiders. Besides, political parties had their own vested interests in organising the tribals. Therefore, the tribal cause on a coordinated fashion was not taken up during this period (Mathur, 1996).

Between 1970 and 1992 the Adivasi Aikya Samithi in Bathery taluk and Adivasi Vikasana Pravarthana Samithi in Vythiri and Manantavady taluks together were formed with a larger vision for tribals of South India. They were inspired by voluntary organisations like SOLIDARITY and High Land Development Association (HILDA), which came out of diocesan social service organisations.

Adivasi Sangamam, 1992

An Adivasi 'Sangamam' (gathering) of tribal organisations of Kerala, Karnataka and Tamil Nadu was organised in October 1992 for eight days. The venue was Manantavady in Wayanad district. Ms. C. K. Janu of Adivasi Vikasana Pravarthaka Samithi (AVPS) was the chairperson of the organising committee with four vice-chairpersons and 14 sub-committees. The programme of the Sangamam consisted of 'Adijyothis' (torch-lit procession) from three states to the venue of the Sangamam. In the Sangamam a national colloquium on various issues of the tribals, exhibition of tribal artefacts, visit to tribal colonies, cultural festival and a cultural procession were held. It was attended by 1,200 Adivasi delegates belonging to 40 communities from eleven states, 300 non-Adivasis and 5,000 tribals. Thus, it was a big event.

There was both opposition to and support for the Sangamam from the public. Yuvajana Vedi of CPI(M) and Bharatiya Janata Party (BJP) opposed the event with a public demonstration, while others protested with statements in the press. There were also organisations which openly supported it. The criticism in the press alleged that the organisers had missionary motive and foreign money.

Adivasi Sangamam, 1993

A South Indian level Sangamam was held at Kodagu, in Karnataka from 12–19 October, 1993. The programmes, like that of the first gathering, consisted of 'adijyothis' (torch lit procession), exhibition of Adivasi artefacts, a colloquium, visit to Adivasi colonies by the delegates, cultural festival and cultural demonstration of about 7,000 participants. Ms. Medha Patkar addressed the rally. However, there was non-cooperation and non-participation from some NGOs and Adivasi organisations.

Adivasi Agitations

The experience of Sangamam made the tribals aware of their problems and rights, which motivated them for action. The Adivasis in Kerala, particularly in Wayanad district organised a number of campaigns on land issues and demanded that the government implement the 'Restriction on Transfer of Land and Restoration of Alienated Lands Act, 1975' but there was no serious response from the government.

On March 1, 1994, the tribals picketed the district Collectorate of Wayanad at Kalpeta under the Adivasi Samyukta Samara Samithi, demanding enforcement of land restoration Act. Earlier they had declared at a public rally in the same town their intention to take over land due to the Adivasis if the government did not do it within a period of three months. However many political parties and farmers' organisations opposed the implementation of the Act.

On the same day, another group of Adivasis under the leadership of Adivasi Aikya Samithi marched to the Cheengeri Project in Sulthan Bathery and later forcefully occupied part of 528 acres of the project land that had been acquired by the government to distribute it to the Adivasis after a period of time but was not distributed even after four decades. The Adivasis were arrested and some of them were remanded to police custody. The Adivasi Aikya Samithi organised a relay hunger-strike for 48 days. A court injunction meanwhile asked the government to keep status quo ante. Most of the Dalit organisations supported the Cheengeri struggle while political parties took an ambivalent stand without supporting or opposing the agitation.

On April 3, 1994, Adivasi Vikasana Pravarthaka Samithi, another Adivasi organisation, marched to a 128-acre vested forest at Ambikutty in Mananthavady and occupied about 67 acres of the land. The forest officials and police tried to evict them and when they resisted, the police attacked them, injuring many. A march to the police station accompanied by rallies and hunger strikes followed. The Collector called for a discussion and assured them of a solution. Based on his assurance the Adivasis stopped the agitation, though he did not fulfil his promise later.

On March 5, 1995, Adivasis marched to 18 acres of revenue land at Panavalli and occupied it by erecting huts and cultivating crops. The forest officials burnt all the houses and arrested some of the Adivasis. They again occupied the land and again got arrested. When they came back from jail they once again occupied the land, but this time they were not evicted.

The reaction of the public towards the struggle of the Adivasis for land was mixed. The political parties took an ambivalent stand depending on whether they were in power or out of power. The intelligentsia were of divergent opinions on the land issue. The farmers in general were opposed to restoration of alienated land of adivasis. The Farmers Relief Forum, an organisation of farmers, though opposed to the Adivasi claim on their alienated land, later supported them in a limited way. The police were totally against Adivasi interests and were even partisan in taking up the cases of Adivasis connected with the agitation.

Struggle for Land Restoration

Even after ten years of various types of struggles, the Adivasis found that the government was not taking any concrete steps to protect their right over the land. They, therefore, resorted to direct action. Under the banner of Adivasi Ekopana Samithi, a vehicle rally was organised from Panavalli in Wayanad to Thiruvananthapuram lasting twenty-two days, to campaign for restoration of Adivasi land. There was good response from people and peoples' organisations for the state-level rally. At the end of the campaign, as the government was planning to introduce a legislation on land issue, a group of women led by C.K. Janu started an indefinite fast in front of the Secretariate, on February 26, 1996. There was also supportive agitation in many district headquarters. As the government did not respond positively to the agitation, on the 13th day of the fast in the morning, Janu, who was very weak in health, was taken inside the Secretariate building. Soon the security guards came and removed her to the hospital. The Chief Minister invited the Adivasi leaders for a talk but as the government did not seem to be serious about it, the Adivasis walked out of the meeting.

On September 23, 1996, the Left Democratic Government passed an amendment bill which legalised all land transactions of the settlers dated till 1986. There were many protests by Dalits, Adivasis and other revolutionary political groups against the Bill, in the form of fast, marches and storming of the State Secretariate. In October of the same year, four young men under the name of 'Ayyankali Pada' took hostage the Collector of Palakkad from morning till evening demanding withdrawal of the amendment to the land Act. The Collector was released at the intervention of prominent citizens. Thereafter, the state government used repressive measures on Adivasis throughout the state alleging extremist activities. The Adivasi Ekopana Samithi, which spearheaded the agitation for restoration of tribal land, publicly disassociated itself from the hostage drama and declared the non-violent nature of their struggle. The Girijan Sevak Samithi, an Adivasi organisation in Attappady in Palakkad district, observed 41-day mourning in protest against the newly enacted bill. At the end of the symbolic action they had the funeral rite for the bill in the Adivasi style. Legal battle, inside and outside the court, and political battle, inside and outside the State Assembly on tribal land issues, went on till 1999, when the government brought out the 'Kerala Restriction on Transfer and Restoration of Lands to Scheduled Tribes Bill', which however it failed to implement.

The next major and much known tribal agitation was in 2001. In response to 32 starvation deaths of tribals reported from various parts of the state, the Adivasi Gothra Maha Sabha, an umbrella organisation of Adivasis in Kerala under the leadership of C.K. Janu and M. Geethanandan launched a state-level agitation in front of the Secretariate in Thiruvananthapuram. They set up several huts in which Adivasis in hundreds from all over the state came and settled for a long time. The agitation received wide support and sympathy from the general public, intellectuals and social organisations. One speciality of the agitation was that Dalits and traditional fishworkers joined hands with the tribals, and so it was named and even known as Adivasi-Dalit Struggle. The government had a series of talks with the tribal leaders, and at the end of 48 days, on October 16, 2001, the Chief Minister along with a few ministers accepted many of the demands of the tribals, the main one being to provide land to all the landless tribals. It was agreed that all the landless Adivasi families would be given land up to five acres within one year depending on the availability of land in each place. The government also agreed to recommend to the President of India to establish tribal self-rule in tribal areas according to the Fifth Schedule and to carry out a master plan for the integrated development of the tribals in the state.

The agreement of the government with the Adivasis was hailed by all as a landmark commitment by any government towards tribal welfare. But the euphoria did not last long as the Chief Minister, A.K. Antony, was not able to implement the accord even after one year. The government distributed only 1,308 acres of land for 568 families while over 40,000 families were still on the waiting list. Land is a vital issue for Adivasis all over India but it is a hot issue in Kerala as the Adivasis are more than ever aware of the broken promises and gross denial of their constitutional rights for the last fifty years. Impatient with the inaction of the government, different tribal organisations including those of political parties started occupying forest and government land in various parts of the state. One example was a group of over 1,000 Adivasis occupying 360 acres of land belonging to the agricultural department at Nelliyampathy in Palakkad district. The encroachment at Muthanga wildlife sanctuary was the most prominent of these land grab agitations. The incident took place in 2003 in the wildlife sanctuary at Muthanga in Wayanad bordering Karnataka and Tamil Nadu. Over 2,000 activists of Adivasi Gothra Mahasabha occupied the protected forest land and were there in temporary huts for 45 days demanding land to the tribals as was promised by the Chief Minister in the previous year. When the police tried to evict the Adivasis from the forest, they resisted it by capturing one policeman and a forest guard, and keeping them in their custody. The massive police force unleashed a brutal attack on the innocent Adivasis and opened fire at them, resulting in the death of an Adivasi and a policeman. Hundreds of Adivasis including women and children were injured or were tortured in jail. Cases were filed against all of them. C.K. Janu and M. Geethanandan, the leaders who had spearheaded the agitation were remanded to police custody though later they were released on bail. The incident was discussed in the Parliament; National Human Rights Commission and SCs/STs Commission took up the issue with the government. The opposition parties and several social organisations organised a series of agitations demanding judicial enquiry. The government, bowing to public pressure, ordered a CBI enquiry, which found lapses in the way the government handled the sensitive situation, but substantially defended the government action.

The Muthanga incident had a dampening effect on the tribals in Kerala. Yet a few instances of forceful occupation of government land have taken place, and the tribal struggle for land is still going on. The government has distributed land to a few hundred more tribal families, the latest being the distribution of one acre of land to 1,717 families from the agricultural farm of the government at Aralam on 22 September 2007 (*Mathrubhumi*, 2007). But, the promise of distribution of land to all landless families still remains a distant dream.

3

Socioeconomic Characteristics of the Tribals

For this study on the effect of globalisation on the tribals in Kerala, the survey method was used with respondents from three districts of Kerala. The questionnaire used for this quantitative study focused on the socioeconomic characteristics of the respondents. The result of the survey which situates the study with the background of the respondents is given in Table 3.1.

Agewise distribution of the respondents shows that 71 per cent of the respondents are in the age groups of 20–39 and 40–49, while the respondents in the age group 30–39 are considerably more than in the other two age groups. A sizeable proportion of the respondents is in the age group of 50–59. The proportion of respondents in the youngest age group and the oldest age group is quite negligible. Among the samples, the coverage of women respondents is also notable (30%). This means that the vast majority of the respondents are mature and knowledgeable persons, and that women are given sizeable representation.

Table 3.1
Background Information of the Tribal Respondents

	Frequency	*Percentage*
SEX		
Male	557	69.9
Female	243	30.4
Total	800	100
AGE (YEARS)		
15–19	12	1.5
20–29	171	21.4
30–39	233	29.1
40–49	165	20.6
50–59	105	13.1
60–69	104	13
80 and above	10	13
Total	800	100
MARITAL STATUS		
Single	41	5.1
Married	666	83.3
Widow	61	7.6
Widower	13	1.6
Divorced	1	0.1
Separated	12	1.5
Unwedded mothers	6	0.5
Total	800	100
EDUCATIONAL LEVEL		
Illiterate	424	53
Drop-out	17	2.1
Literate	95	11.9
Lower Primary	96	12
Upper Primary	85	10.6
High School	71	8.9
Plus2/PUC and above	12	1.5
Total	800	100

About the *marital status* of the respondents, a substantial percentage of the respondents are married (83%). Only a small proportion of the respondents are unmarried (5%). A considerably greater proportion of the respondents are widows (8%) compared to widowers (2%). The proportion of respondents having marital separation is greater (2%) compared with that of divorced and unwedded mothers. Unwedded mothers among the tribals are only a small percentage (0.5%), that too from Wayanad.

The educational level of the respondents shows that more than half (53%), are reported to be illiterate. However, a considerable proportion of the respondents (37%), is either educated up to primary level or upper primary level. This is also evident in the case of respondents who are just literate. Altogether, 26 per cent are educated up to primary level compared to those who are educated up to upper primary level. On the other hand, a considerable proportion is educated up to high school level. The proportion of respondents educated beyond high school level is quite small. Similar is the proportion of dropouts. Considering the low educational level of the tribals, there is a good mix of literate and illiterate respondents.

Occupational distribution of the respondents highlights that about three-fifths are coolies and a good proportion is small farmers (16%). On the other hand, the proportion reported to be unemployed is also sizeable (15%). The proportion of respondents in the other occupational categories is negligible. However, a small proportion is either semi-government or government employees. Normally the tribal groups are supposed to gather forest products besides their routine work but this study shows that only a negligible proportion is engaged in such work (1%). Unlike in olden times, today forest is no longer a source of livelihood for tribals in India, particularly in Kerala.

Monthly income of the respondents from agriculture indicates that 69 per cent do not have any monthly income from agriculture. However, notably larger proportion of the respondents are having monthly income of less than rupees 500 compared to those in higher categories of monthly income. The proportion of respondents having monthly income above Rs 501 is negligible. On the, other hand, only a small proportion of respondents (24%) has monthly income from non-agriculture as compared to those with income from agriculture (nearly one-third).

Table 3.2
Occupation and Income of the Tribal Respondents

	Frequency	*Percentage*
Occupation of the Respondents		
Unemployed	117	14.6
Coolies	473	59.1
Farmers	126	15.8
Technicians	4	0.5
Clerks	1	0.1
Government employees	14	1.8
Collectors of forest produce	10	1.3
Petty business	2	0.3
Coolie + farmers	30	3.8
Others	23	2.9
Total	800	100
Monthly Income from Agriculture (in Rupees)		
No income	551	68.9
Below 500	176	22
501–1000	43	5.4
1001–1500	23	2.8
1501 and above	7	0.9
Total	800	100
Monthly Income from Non-agriculture (in Rupees)		
No income	192	24
Below 500	349	43.6
501–1000	216	27
1001–1500	24	3
1501–2000	5	0.6
2000 and above	14	1.8
Total	800	100

Pattern of savings among the respondents reveals that about 80 per cent reported not to be saving any money. A significant proportion of the respondents save their money through self-help groups and 'kudumbashree' which are mainly meant for women (11%). Even among those having saving, the annual saving is below rupees 500.

Table 3.3
Pattern of Savings of the Tribal Respondents

	No. of Respondents	*Percentage*
Pattern of Savings of the Respondents (in Rupees)		
No savings	643	80.4
Chits/funds	5	0.6
Cooperative society	6	0.8
Post-office savings	5	0.6
Bank deposit	10	1.3
Self-help group	47	5.8
Kudumbhashree	72	9
Others	12	1.5
Total	800	100
Annual Savings of the Respondents (in Rupees)		
No savings	635	79.4
Below 500	89	11.1
501–1000	36	4.5
1001–1500	8	1
1501–2000	6	0.8
2001–2500	26	3.3
Total	800	100

Social participation of the respondents shows that 61 per cent have not participated in any kind of social groups. A sizeable proportion has participated in political activities (15%), followed by 'kudumbashree' and Self-help groups supported by the Panchayat (10%). A comparatively greater percentage have participated in cooperative societies (4%).

Table 3.4
Social Participation of the Tribal Respondents

Type of Social Participation of the Respondents	*No. of Respondents*	*Percentage*
Nil	486	60.8
Political parties	121	15.1
Arts and sports club	11	1.4
Cooperative society	35	4.4
Mahila Samaj	2	0.3
Self-help groups (SHGs)	28	3.5
Kudumbhashree	80	10
Cooperative society and Kudumbhashree	8	1
Self-help groups and Kudumbhashree	26	3.3
Others	3	0.4
Total	800	100

Health status of the respondents reveals that quite a large percentage of the respondents reported to be in good health (87%) However, a considerably greater proportion reported to be having rheumatic fever and asthma (6%), compared to those who have other kinds of health problems.

Table 3.5
Health Status of the Tribal Respondents

Health Status of the Respondents	*No. of Respondents*	*Percentage*
Handicapped	6	0.8
Blind	5	0.6
Deaf	2	0.3
Dumb	1	0.1
TB patient	4	0.5
Cancer Patient	2	0.3
Rheumatic fever	34	4.3
Diabetes	5	0.6
Asthma	14	1.8
Sickle anaemia	1	0.1
Others	699	3.4
No illness	27	87.4
Total	800	100

Details regarding *housing* show that 59 per cent of the respondents have house sites of less than ten cents, and the proportion having house site of higher size is notably small. For example, 10 per cent of the respondents have house sites between 26–50 cents. It is necessary to mention here that the size of land for a house site stated in cents for most of the respondents includes cultivable land, since the land pattern in Kerala is usually of a house inside a farm.

Table 3.6

Housing and its Amenities of the Tribal Respondents

Description	*Number of Respondents*	*Percentage*
Size of land for house sites (in cents)		
Below 10	472	59.0
11–25	71	8.9
26–50	82	10.3
51–100	53	6.6
101–250	67	8.4
251–500	49	6.1
501 and above	6	0.8
Total	800	100
Nature of house sites of tribals		
Own land	281	35.1
Without title deed	8	1.0
Rehabilitated area	78	9.8
Tenancy	15	1.9
Forest area	106	13.3
Joint ownership	147	18.4
Own land, without title deed in forest land	165	20.6
Total	800	100
Type of house of tribals		
Concrete house	27	3.4
Tiled house	475	59.4
Thatched house	204	25.5
Asbestos-roofed house	94	11.8
Total	800	100

Cont'd...

Cont'd...

Availability of electricity connection in the house		
No	642	80.3
Yes	158	19.7
Total	800	100
Use of solar energy		
No	572	71.5
Yes	228	28.5
Total	800	100
Source of solar energy		
Not using	574	71.8
From government	220	27.5
From NGO	6	0.8
Total	800	100
Availability of latrine facility in the house		
No	575	71.9
Yes	225	28.1
Total	800	100
Type of latrine facility		
Not applicable	575	71.9
Septic	121	15.1
Public latrine	13	1.6
Pit latrine	91	11.4
Total	800	100
Sources of drinking water		
Own well	17	2.1
Public well	367	45.9
Public tap	137	17.1
Stream	63	7.9
Small pond	159	19.9
Other sources	57	7.1
Total	800	100
Possession of household articles		
No articles	435	54.4

Cont'd...

Cont'd...

Kerosene stove	4	0.5
Smokeless choolas	13	1.6
Bicycle	7	0.9
Radio	242	30.3
Tape recorder	35	4.4
Television	9	1.1
Gas	2	0.3
Smokeless choolas and radio	3	0.4
Radio and tape recorder	47	5.9
Radio, television and cooking gas	3	0.4
Total	800	100

Ownership of the house site of the respondents indicates that only 35 per cent claimed that it is their own land. A notable proportion (21%) also claimed it as their own land, but it is without title deed in the forest, as is the case with Muthuvans in Idukki district. Another 18 per cent claimed that their land is owned jointly by more than one household. Fifty-nine per cent of the households have tiled house and one-fourth has thatched house. A considerable proportion of the respondents also has houses with asbestos roof (12%). On the other hand, only a small proportion of the respondents has concrete houses (3%). Seventy-four per cent have pucca houses, if we add together those having tiled, concrete and asbestos houses. This is due to the government housing scheme by which they get a subsidy up to Rs 40,000. Muthuvans and Ulladars of Idukki district have mostly thatched houses (90% and 80% respectively), since they live in interior forest land.

Regarding other housing amenities, the situation of tribals is very pathetic. The study reveals that 80 per cent of houses do not have electricity in their house in a state which claims to be totally electrified. A notable proportion of the respondents stated that they have been provided with solar energy for their use (29%), which is mainly sponsored by government schemes. Mostly the Muthuvans of Idukki district, who live in forest land, use solar energy, as forest policy does not allow them to take electric line to the forest area. Similarly, almost three-fourths (72%) of the tribals do not have toilet facilities. It is worth noting that the main source of drinking water for the respondents is the public well (46%). This is followed by those using small ponds (20%). A sizeable proportion uses the public tap. If we add up those who have access to public well and public tap, a vast majority (63%) of the tribals in Kerala get drinking water from public water supply, which is good enough compared to the situation of the state as a whole.

With regard to possession of household articles, the study indicates that majority of the tribal families do not have any articles of luxury (54%). On the other hand, a notable proportion has radio (36%) if we add radio cum-tape-recorder. One notable characteristic in Kerala is easy availability of non-essential consumer goods like television, washing machine, motorcycles, cooking gas etc., which the middle class avail themselves of. But many luxury consumer goods which can be said to be the product of globalisation are not used by the tribals. In other words, tribals are not beneficiaries of luxury goods like television and mobile phone which are very much linked to globalisation.

4

Impact of Globalisation on the Livelihood of the Tribals

Livelihood is basic to people in any country. Globalisation is supposed to be a process which is to give proper means of livelihood to all and thus ensure a better standard of living. This study aims at finding out the impact of globalisation on the livelihood of tribals, the poorest section of society in Kerala.

The study examines some areas of livelihood which are immediately relevant for the tribals in Kerala. They are land, employment, wages, and availability of essential commodities. In order to find out whether globalisation has had some effect on the tribals, the study makes a comparison between the situation before the globalisation process started in India and that which existed after it was started. As explained in the first chapter, the year 1991 is approximately taken in this study as the year in which the reform for globalisation was introduced in India, and so comparison is made between the period before 1991, termed in this study as pre-reform period, and the ten year period after 1991, termed in this study as post-reform period, till the study was conducted in 2003. To make it easy for the tribals the question was asked about the situation of the identified areas ten years ago and at present, i.e. at the time of the study. They were also asked about the reasons for change, if at all there is a change, between the present situation and situation ten years back.

Land and Cultivation

Land is one of the means of production for all economic activities. All the more so for tribals, the weakest section of the population in Kerala, whose livelihood, life and culture are closely bound up with land. Besides, most tribals in Kerala were deprived of land over the years, as was shown in an earlier chapter. So here an analysis is made about the situation of land owned by the tribals in Kerala.

Table 4.1

Land Use and Cultivation of Tribals in Kerala Ten Years Ago and at Present

Description	*Ten years ago*		*At present*	
	Number of Respondents	*%age*	*Number of Respondents*	*%age*
Possession of Farm Land by Tribals				
No	484	60.5	473	59.1
Yes	316	39.5	327	40.9
4.1B Cultivable land owned by tribals (in acres)				
No land	484	60.5	473	59.1
0.1–1	127	15.9	147	18.4
1.1–2	83	10.4	85	10.6
2.1–4	75	9.4	68	8.5
4.1 and above	31	3.9	27	3.4
4.1C Nature of cultivation				
No cultivation	484	60.5	473	59.1
Subsistence farming	274	34.0	124	15.5
Commercial	26	3.3	174	21.8
Subsistence and commercial farming	16	2.5	29	3.6

The study reveals that a vast majority of the respondents at present (59%) does not possess land. This corroborates the secondary data given earlier about land situation of tribals in Kerala. The situation ten years back is much the same (61%), meaning that globalisation as such is not a reason for dispossession of land by tribals.

Among those who have land, a sizeable section (34%) had subsistence farming ten years back, viz., cultivation for their own use and not for market. But this has decreased by more than half (16%) at present. On the other hand commercial farming among tribals has increased to 22 per cent at present compared to 3 per cent ten years back. If we consider these two data of substantial increase in commercial farming and substantial decrease in subsistent farming at present compared to the situation ten years back, it shows increasing dependence of tribals on market during post-reform period. It is possible that tribals went for commercial farming in order to get additional income needed for essential commodities and services, and that market economy driven by globalisation has influenced the tribals to go for commercial farming.

Case studies of three villages of Paliyakudy in Idukki district, Mully in Palakkad district and Marakadavu in Wayanad district confirm the findings of the survey study on land cultivation. Though more than half of these villages have land, the size is less than 50 cents that too often owned by joint families. This size is obviously very small for a viable cultivation. In many cases the land is dry, which can be cultivated only with sufficient rain as there is no irrigation facility. For example at Mully village 90 per cent of tribal land is dry and can be cultivated only with rain, which is rare in the area. At Marakadavu there is only 5.50 acres of land for 106 families, which comes to eight cents of land per family. It is again too small to be a source of income. The problem becomes acute when such a small plot of land is divided among adult members of the family to construct separate houses. This means that land is not a source of financial support even for those who have some land.

Table 4.2

Types of Cash Crops Cultivated by the Tribals in Kerala

Types of Cash Crops	*Yes*		*No*	
Coconut	78	9.7	722	90.3
Cardamom	59	7.4	741	92.6
Pepper	145	18.1	655	81.9
Ginger	55	6.9	745	93.1
Coffee	126	15.8	674	84.3
Turmeric	43	5.4	757	94.6

Crop pattern here is broadly categorised for two major crops, namely cash crops and food crops. It can be seen from the table that out of the total land owners, only 24 per cent are reported to be cultivating coconut, while a large proportion are reported to be cultivating pepper (44%) followed by coffee (39%). The proportion of those who cultivated cardamom, ginger and turmeric is notably small (18, 17, and 13 per cent respectively).

There is an increasing tendency also among tribals from these villages to cultivate cash crops. The implication of this tendency is that the tribals who were depending on food crops from their own land in earlier times, now depend on market economy as their land is not providing them with food crops.

Table 4.3

Types of Food Crops Cultivated by Tribals in Kerala

Types of Food Crops	*Yes*		*No*	
Plantain	150	18.8	650	81.3
Paddy	78	9.8	722	90.3
Vegetables	67	8.4	733	91.6
Ragi	170	21.3	630	78.8
Corn	57	7.1	743	92.9
Tapioca	151	18.9	649	81.1

The food crop pattern shows that more than half of the respondents (52%) are reported to be cultivating ragi followed by those who cultivated plantain (46%) and tapioca (47%). The proportion of those who cultivated paddy, vegetables and maize is notably small (24%, 21% and 17% respectively). The life of the tribals is getting commercialised and they are purchasing all commodities of their daily needs from the market. Commercialisation of the non-commercial life of the tribals has deprived them of their sources of life.

Among the villages selected for case study only Paliyakudy in Idukki district had some income from forest. Here, 75 per cent of tribals got some income from forest produce like honey and firewood. But even in this village there is increasing pressure from the World Bank sponsored Eco-development Project functioning in the village, not to use forest products. It has the stated objective of decreasing the dependence of tribals on forest and its income. To achieve this, the project provides self-employment programmes, bank loans and Self-Help Groups (SHGs) as alternative sources of income.

Employment and Income

The study has already analysed how land, which was the main source of livelihood for the tribals in Kerala, was lost to them and how it ceased to be a means of livelihood. When the tribals lost their land, the next means available for them was wage labour in the farmlands mostly of non-tribals and even of upper caste people. They worked in plantations of cash crops and paddy fields as coolie workers. This section examines whether globalisation has affected the employment and wages of the tribals. For this the study explores the situation of employment and wages in pre-reform and post-reform period, concretely at present and ten years back.

Table 4.4

Employment and Wage Details of Tribals Ten Years Ago and at Present

Description	*10 years ago*				*At present*			
	Male		*Female*		*Male*		*Female*	
	Nos.	*%*	*Nos.*	*%*	*Nos.*	*%*	*Nos.*	*%*
No. of Working Days								
No work	197	24.6	237	29.6	166	20.8	232	29.0
Below 50	89	11.1	123	15.4	185	23.1	311	38.9
51–100	38	4.8	57	7.1	235	29.4	157	19.6
101–200	181	22.6	246	30.8	185	23.1	88	11.0
201–300	268	33.5	128	16.0	29	3.6	12	1.5
300 and above	27	3.4	9	1.1				
Daily Wages								
No wages	197	24.6	237	29.6	166	20.8	232	29.0
Below 25	87	10.9	174	21.8	61	7.6	362	45.3
26–50	202	25.3	361	45.1	565	70.6	203	25.4
51–100	310	38.8	28	3.5	8	1.0	3	0.4
100 and above	4	0.5						

The survey study examined the situation of working days per year to analyse employment, which is the most crucial means of livelihood for the tribals. As in the case of earlier data, enquiry was made through survey schedule as to the employment situation in pre-reform period which was taken as the period before 1991, and post-reform period till the year of this study, i.e., in 2003. The employment situation of tribals 10 years after structural adjustment programme was introduced is likely to show how globalisation has affected the situation of tribals in Kerala.

According to the table the highest rate of employment per year among men 10 years back was 36 per cent with the number of working days ranging from 201–300. It reveals that these men had more than 200 days of work ten years back. In contrast, at present only 4 per cent men have working days above 200 days. A relatively greater proportion of men (29%) have fallen to the 51–100 range of working days in a year at present, while this rate of employment was only 5 per cent ten years back. The average working days calculated from this table for men per year is 135 days ten years back, while at present it is 72 days. This is all the more striking as the study shows that 21 per cent of men at present are without work. This means there is a drastic decrease in the number of working days per year for men between pre-reform period and post-reform period.

With regard to the employment of tribal women the table shows that 31 per cent had employment ranging from 101–200 ten years back while only 11 per cent of women come in that range at present. In contrast, 39 per cent of women have come down to the range below 50 days of work compared to 15 per cent in the same range ten years back. The average working days calculated from this table for women per year ten years back was 99 while it is 45 at present. This means there is considerable decrease in the working days of women per year in the post-reform period. This is all the more glaring when 29 per cent of women are shown by the study to be unemployed at present.

The second part of the table above shows the wage rate of men and women per day ten years back and at present. There is variation of wage for both men and women. The wage range of Rs 51–100 was received by 39 per cent of men ten years ago while at present only 8 per cent of men receive that high wage. On the other hand 71 per cent of men received a wage range of Rs 26–50 at present, while only 25 per cent of them received the same range of wage ten years back.

Wage for 45 per cent of women was in the range of Rs 26–50 ten years back while the same range has been reduced to 25 per cent at present. On the other hand 22 per cent of women got a wage range below Rs 25, while the same rate is for 45 per cent at present. This means less women get a higher level of wage while more women have come down to a lower range of wage. It is to be noted from the study that tribal women in general were paid much lower wage than men. This factor, together with decrease in number of working days, has made women more dependent on men's meagre income than in the pre-reform period.

The main reason for drastic decrease in employment and marginal reduction in wages for both men and women given by the respondents in the personal interviews was that land owners did not have much work in their plantation. The reason for this, according to the respondents themselves, was crash in price of cash crops during the last ten years of reform period. The low price for crops was further attributed to import of the same produce from other countries. Palakkad district has less unemployment problem compared to Wayanad district because the Japanese funded Attapady Hill Area Development Society (AHADS) project has created a number of job opportunities for tribals through afforestation programs.

Employment was found to be a crucial problem for the villages chosen for the case study. At Marakadavu in Wayanad district the average working days for men was 100–120 days in a year while in earlier years they were getting 250–300 days. Some people got work connected with ginger cultivation at Coorgu in Karnataka on a seasonal basis but its scope was limited depending on the price of ginger. Earlier, Adivasis used to get supplementary income from forests but this source is totally closed at present due to the destruction of forests and implementation of forest laws. As a result of the low rate of employment, 100 out of 106 women at Marakadavu who are members of 'Kudumbashree' do not have any money to deposit in the scheme. A few years back there were a number of deaths in this tribal village due to starvation. Then the government and other agencies came to help the village through free ration and medical facilities. The free ration has been stopped now, though medical services are being continued; so the possibility of death is prevented. But the study revealed that very few families in the colony have one meal a day. Unless some urgent steps are taken to provide employment or land, there is possibility of more starvation deaths in the future too.

The same story is repeated at Mully in Palakkad district. One hundred tribals worked in the nearby tea estate ten years back, but now only ten people get work there. The reason is low price of tea with the result of less work in the tea estates. Some young people there were getting jobs in textile mills in Coimbatore, but since many of the factories have closed down they have lost their jobs.

All the three villages chosen for case study reported that there was no decrease in real wages during the last ten years. However there was no increase in wages either. This means that the economic situation and consequent quality of life is worse than it was ten years back if rise of price of essential commodities is taken into account since. With the same wage the tribals would not be getting the same quantity and quality of food as they used to get in the past. Besides, the considerable decrease in the number of working days during the last ten years has added to the woes of the tribals.

Wayanad has the highest rate of unemployment among the tribals in Kerala. It is also the most affected district for loss of working days during the last ten years since the increasing shift from food crops to commercial crops in the region has decreased the working days for tribals. Thus, for example, arecanut—a cash crop—requires less regular work than paddy, the labour for which can also provide wage in kind, viz. paddy itself. It was further accentuated during the last few years as is shown in the study. Palakkad districts in the study also have serious problems of unemployment which stands at 44 per cent. But here it is mitigated by the Japan financed Attapady Hills Area Development Society (AHADS) project which provides work for many tribals in major colonies through programmes like watershed and afforestation.

Availability of Essential Commodities

This chapter has so far examined land and employment as means of livelihood for tribals in Kerala. It found that they are no longer sufficient means for their livelihood. As a welfare measure the government has been giving subsidised food materials especially to the marginalised groups through ration shops and other forms of public distribution system, which has been a great support and source of food security for them. The tribals, the most marginalised community in Kerala, were very much dependent on the public distribution system for their essential commodities to supplement their meagre income from employment and land. Therefore, the study has analysed whether the essential commodities are available at present for the tribals, and if not, what are the reasons for such a situation. It has also examined what essential commodities the tribals regularly use, and the sources from which they get these commodities. In this section, the respondents were asked about the sources of daily food, possession of ration cards, its use for buying essential commodities and the use of non-essential commodities like alcohol and tobacco.

Table 4.5
Possession of Ration Card by Tribals

No	*%age*	*Yes*	*%age*
136	17	664	83

Table 4.6
Use of Ration Card by Tribals for Buying Essential Commodities

No	*%age*	*Yes*	*%age*	*No Ration Card*	*%age*
48	6	616	77	136	17

Access to food is one of the basic human rights, and the respondents were asked whether they were having ration card to get essential commodities such as rice, sugar and kerosene given through the ration shops in India. It was found that a substantial proportion of the respondents had ration cards (83%) and the remaining did not have ration cards. A considerable proportion of those not having ration card facility (17%) said that they were migrants or recently settled families. The ration cardholders were asked whether they purchased essential commodities regularly from ration shops or not. Most of the ration cardholders (93%) replied that they regularly purchased the essential commodities from the ration shop.

Table 4.7
Reasons for Not Using Ration Card by Tribals for Buying Essential Commodities

	No. of Respondents	*Percentage*
Not applicable	752	94
High prices	8	1
Lack of good quality	7	0.9
Others	2	0.3
High price and availability of quality rice with same price	31	39

This table gives the reasons the respondents gave for not going to ration shops for purchasing essential commodities. Those who did not buy food materials from ration shops gave the combined reasons of high price and low quality (39%). Though only a small section of respondents subscribed to this, it points to a prevalent situation confirmed by case studies and secondary data, that tribals increasingly go to private shops due to low quality and high price of essential commodities in ration shops. This is also indicated in the sources of essential commodities given in the following table.

According to the data, only a small per cent of tribals buy non-vegetarian items like fish and meat. Seventy-nine per cent do not buy it at all. It is surprising that in Kerala where fish is a major source of protein for majority of people, it is not eaten by the tribals, depriving them of a rich protein food. But the role of ration shop is only evident in the case of respondents' access to essential commodities including cereals, sugar and kerosene. A majority of the respondents (57%) purchased cereals from private shops compared to those who purchased it from ration shops (40%). More or less similar proportion get sugar and kerosene both from ration and private shops (49%). This is a clear indication that the tribals depend more and more on private shops for essential commodities unlike earlier times, due to high price and low quality.

Case studies also confirms the data about sources of essential commodities mentioned above. At Marakadavu in Wayanad district as was shown earlier, there is hardly any land for cultivation. Even in the tiny plots of land they possess collectively, they cultivate cash crops. The same is true of Paliyakudy in Idukky district where they get some income from forest. In the village of Mully in Palakkad district some food crops, viz., ragi, maize, grams, etc. are cultivated depending on the rain. Otherwise the tribals are also very much dependent on the public distribution system.

This chapter examined data on the impact of globalisation on the livelihood of the tribals in Kerala. The means of livelihood of tribals chosen for the study are land, employment, wages, and availability of essential commodities. The study examined the condition of these means at present in comparison with the pre-reform period to show the impact of globalisation on tribal life with regard to these means of livelihood. It was found that dispossession of land by the tribals did not take place in the post-reform period, and so is not related to

Table 4.8

Sources of Essential Commodities for Tribals

Sources	*Cereals*		*Grams*		*Tuber Crops*		*Milk Products*		*Meat/Fish*		*Sugar/Kerosene*	
	Users	*%*	*Users*	*%*	*Users*	*%*	*Users*	*%*	*Users*	*%*	*Users*	*%*
Not regularly purchased	—	—	101	12.6	410	51.3	703	87.9	632	79.0	17	2.1
Ration shop	318	39.8	—	—	—	—	—	—	—	—	390	48.8
Private shop	454	56.8	669	83.6	330	41.3	73	9.1	163	20.4	393	49.1
Own farm	28	3.5	30	3.8	55	6.9	24	3.0	5	0.6	—	—
Forest	—	—	—	—	5	0.6	—	—	—	—	—	—

globalisation. But since they had lost their land long ago, post-reform period made their life extremely miserable as they were deprived of one important source of livelihood. The study revealed that employment got reduced drastically in the post-reform period compared to pre-reform period, meaning globalisation may have affected employment, the main means of livelihood for the tribals in Kerala.

Though the wages were not drastically cut, the fact that there was no increase in real wages in the post-reform period implies that the tribals were badly affected in view of increase in prices of commodities and decrease in the number of working days. Thus their income was reduced considerably leading to less money to spend for their essential needs. More than half of the tribals depend on private shops for essential food grains at present. With the increase in prices of commodities it is possible that globalisation has forced the tribals to depend more and more on private shops for their essential needs.

5

Impact of Globalisation on the Sociocultural Life of the Tribals

Though globalisation normally deals with the economic life of people in a country it also influences their religio-cultural life. As more and more economic interdependence and integration is taking place among countries there is apprehension in many people today that cultures could also be affected through values and culture of western countries which very much dominate the world. This study on the impact of globalisation on the tribals in Kerala, also examines its impact on the cultural and religious practices of the tribals. Culture in this study means the sum-total of customs, life style, symbols and value system of a people. The study includes religion, education and status of women since they are closely linked with culture, especially in a tribal community. As was done for the livelihood of the tribals, this chapter examines the present situation of culture and religious practices of the tribals in comparison that with that of the pre-reform period to see whether the policies and programmes of globalisation have affected these areas of the tribals or not. As part of cultural life, data about the present situation of education of tribal children, health, and status of tribal women are also presented. Thus this chapter deals with four sections—impact of globalisation on culture and religious practices, health, education and status of tribal women.

Impact of Globalisation on the Cultural and Religious Practices of the Tribals in Kerala

In the following table, changes occurring through television and cinema in family and customs, tribal values like sharing and cooperation, and reasons for loss of tribal values are dealt with. Television channels are not only visual media of communication but are also means of advertising very effectively consumer goods of local and foreign companies. They are very powerful in influencing the values, life style and culture of people. Thus television networks can be taken as a symbolic expression of privatisation and globalisation. In this section their effect on tribal life is examined. Since cinema also operates in a similar way, it is also added to television.

The respondents were asked about the impact of globalisation on the cultural life of tribals. The first question asked was whether television and cinema had any impact on tribal family and customs. Half of the respondents (51%) stated that they had impacted on their family and customs. Among them, 17 per cent stated that modern life style had influenced their life, 19 per cent stated that it brought about changes in fashions, food, language and behaviour, and 14 per cent stated that it brought combined changes in fashions, dressing, language and food pattern. A considerable proportion of the respondents stated that it brought about changes in food pattern (6%). To know about changes in the traditional values of tribal community like sharing, common ownership and cooperation, a question was asked to the respondents whether any decline had occurred in the above-mentioned traditional values. Forty-three per cent respondents reported that there had been a decline in their traditional values. Among the respondents who noticed such changes, a considerably large proportion stated that this was because of emergence of nuclear family (9%), or because of changes in behaviour (9%). According to another 17 per cent this was because of selfishness and addiction to liquor.

Table 5.1
Impact of Globalisation on the Cultural Life of Tribals in Kerala

Description	*Number of Respondents*	*Percentage*
Changes on family and customs of the tribals through TV and cinema		
No	396	49.5
Yes	406	50.5
Areas of tribal life affected through TV and cinema		
No change	396	49.5
Influence of modern life style	139	17.4
Change in food pattern	44	5.5
Change in fashion, dressing, language and food pattern	66	8.3
Different factors in combination	108	13.6
Influence of media	47	5.9
Total	800	100
Loss of tribal values like sharing, common ownership and cooperation		
No	458	57.3
Yes	342	42.8
Total	800	100
Reasons for loss of tribal values like sharing, common ownership and cooperation		
No change	458	57.3
Change in behaviour	68	8.6
Emergence of nuclear family	74	9.2
Lack of collective action	25	3.1
Poverty and selfishness	40	5.0
Poverty, selfishness and liquor	41	5.1
Selfishness and liquor	52	6.5
Other reasons	42	5.2
Total	800	100

Case studies also confirmed that tribal customs and practices were negatively affected by television and cinema. In the village of Mully in Palakkad district people used to watch video films throughout the night for days together so that 'Koothu', the main cultural form, had totally gone out of practice. They also reported that the tribals were so influenced by values and lifestyles of non-tribals that tribal values like cooperation and sharing had diminished. At Paliyakudy in Idukki district, a traditional dance form and rituals connected with death are the only surviving practices among tribals. The tribals strongly felt that modern life had destroyed all their customs so much that the modern generation of tribals do not even accept them as their own.

Both at Mully and Paliyakudy it was reported that advertisements on television and films had tremendously increased the desire of tribals to buy all sorts of commodities, leading to consumerism. This can means that tribals spend most of their meagre income on non-essential commodities, curtailing the consumption of essential food items. Since advertisements in electronic media are very much part of globalisation, tribals become victims of the evil effects of globalisation. At Paliyakudy many tribals got into debt trap by buying all kinds non-essential consumer goods. This adversely affected the quality of life of tribals regarding education, food and shelter. Thus development due to globalisation seems to have lowered the quality of life of the tribals.

Culture and religion are closely related, especially among indigenous people. Therefore, this study enquired about the effect of globalisation on some of the religious practices of tribals. In this section changes or loss in some religious practices of tribals in Kerala in recent years and the reasons for such changes are considered.

To know about the impact of globalisation on religious practices of tribals, questions were asked whether the tribals had lost any of their religious practices in recent years. More than half of the respondents (55%) expressed their opinion that they had lost many of their religious practices in recent years. Among the respondents who felt such loss in their religious practices, a notably great proportion reported that they had lost the religious practices related to birth and death (17%). Another considerable proportion stated that they had lost religious practices and cultural activities (17%), followed by those who noticed loss of practices related to marriage (11%).

Table 5.2

Impact of Globalisation on Religious Practices of Tribals in Kerala

Description	*Number of Respondents*	*Percentage*
Loss of any religious practices of tribals in recent years		
No	364	45.5
Yes	436	54.5
Total	800	100
Tribal religious practices which are lost in recent years		
No response	364	45.5
Marriage customs	89	11.1
Religious rituals	33	4.1
Religious customs related to birth and death	136	17.0
Religious practices and cultural activities	137	17.1
Customs related to farming	41	5.2
Total	800	100
Loss of interest in the new generation of tribals in religious practices		
No	343	42.9
Yes	457	57.1
Total	800	100
Reasons for loss of interest in religious practices among the new generation		
Not applicable	343	42.9
They have not imbibed the old practices	58	7.3
They have adjusted to new life style	54	6.8
They consider the old practices bad/irrelevant/expensive	25	3.1
Inferiority complex of tribals	46	5.8
They have not imbibed the old and adjusted to new life style	87	10.9
They have not imbibed the old rituals, and inferiority complex	52	6.5
They are adjusted to new life, and rituals are expensive	24	3.0
They consider them bad or irrelevant, and inferiority complex of tribals	21	2.6
They have not imbibed the old practices, adjusted to new life, and inferiority complex of tribals	39	4.9
They have not imbibed the old rituals, they are expensive, inferiority complex of tribals and other reasons	51	6.4
Total	800	100

Case studies of three villages have also confirmed that the tribals have lost many religious practices in the recent past. Among tribals of Wayanad folklore dance and other cultural practices were reported to have been lost. Among the Muthuvans of Idukki there is the custom of keeping girls and boys in confinement when they reach adulthood. This is slowly disappearing as the tribals themselves realise that it prevents the children from continuing school education. Also they had the custom of keeping pregnant women in a 'satram' (rest houses) till their delivery and aftercare. It was a good custom of giving special care to them. But when there is complication in delivery, they are not able to cope with it. Now they are slowly replacing this custom with modern treatment in the hospital. 'Kani' or 'Moopan', the traditional system of leadership among the tribals, is losing its hold among them. If the tribal self-rule is allowed, their traditional leadership with the traditional structure of 'oorukootam' could be retained by removing its drawbacks and integrating the good elements of modern democratic process.

Another question asked to the respondents was about the observance of traditional religious practices by the new generation. The respondents were asked whether the new generation was losing interest in religious practices. More than a half of the respondents (57%) reported in the affirmative. The reasons for the loss of their interest as reported by the respondents were that the new generation had not imbibed the old practices and was getting adjusted to a new lifestyle (11%), followed by the reason that they had not imbibed the old practices (7%). Other important reasons cited were: they have adjusted to a new lifestyle and have not imbibed the old rituals, and are having are inferiority complex about their traditional practices (12% and 11% respectively). A considerable proportion stated the reason of inferiority complex (10%) and the combined reasons of not assimilating old practices, getting adjusted to new life and inferiority complex (9%).

According to the study, the tribals themselves are of the opinion that globalisation through its powerful channels of television and cinema has adversely affected their culture and religious practices. They are afraid that their culture may be even destroyed or subsumed by the overpowering mainstream culture very much controlled by the process of globalisation. Similarly, the tribal respondents expressed the fear that their traditional religious practices would soon be lost as a result of the influence of globalisation and its vehicles of communication media.

Impact of Globalisation on Health Status of the Tribals in Kerala

Good health is a basic requirement for the development of a people. It is the duty of the state to provide medical facilities for its citizens, as has been done so far by the government. But with the advent of globalisation there is increasing entry of private institutions for medical education and treatment. As the weaker sections like the tribals and the Dalits are not able to depend on private institutions, there is high risk for the health of these communities today. So this section examines the impact of globalisation on the health status of the tribals in Kerala. This is done by studying the health status through nature of death, immunisation status and use of liquor, and the situation of health services of tribals ten years back and at present.

The study shows that most of the household members of the respondents (87%), are in good health condition (Table 3.5). Only a negligible proportion of the household members were reported to be suffering from some kind of disease or are handicapped. Though the proportion is quite small, the number of household members suffering from rheumatic fever and other diseases is notable. Special attention needs to be given to the treatment of these diseases.

Table 5.3

Nature of Death of the Tribals in Kerala

Nature of Death	*Numbers*	*Percentage*
No death during last 10 years	259	32.4
Old age death	370	46.3
Sudden death	117	14.6
Suicide	11	1.4
Murder	3	0.4
Accidental death	8	1
Unnatural death	2	0.3
Infant mortality	23	2.9
Sudden death and infant mortality	7	0.9

The table indicates the type of death occurring among the tribals during the last ten years. Out of the 800 respondents, 32 per cent of the respondents' families did not have any deaths at all during the last ten years. Among the respondents who had deaths in their families, 46 per cent stated that they were due to old age, which was followed by 15 per cent stating incidence of sudden death. A small proportion (3%) reported infant mortality and a further proportion reported other causes of death such as suicide, murder and accidental death. Low incidence of death is an indicator of good health corroborating good health index of the tribals mentioned above.

Table 5.4
Immunisation Status of Tribal Children in Kerala

Status of Immunisation	*Numbers*	*Percentage*
No	49	6.1
Yes	397	49.6
Do not know	354	44.3

It is essential to know about the knowledge of tribals regarding immunisation of children, since it is a basic preventive health measure. Only 50 per cent of the respondents stated that their children had been immunised. A small proportion (6%) stated that their children had not got immunised while pathetically 44 per cent of the respondents did not know about immunisation of their children. The reason for ignorance of such a large proportion of the tribal respondents about immunisation could be that there is neither government nor non-governmental organisation to make them aware of the need of immunisation and to implement immunisation programmes effectively among them. Palakkad had the lowest awareness about immunisation, especially the Mudugars and Irulars.

Table 5.5
Use of Liquor/Drugs by Tribals in Kerala

	Numbers	*Percentage*
No	381	47.6
Yes	419	52.4

Constant use of liquor/drugs can ruin the physical and mental health of the tribals, in addition to breaking the sociocultural unity of their families and the community. In the case of respondents' personal habits such as use of liquor and drugs, a little more than half reported to be using liquor or drugs (52%). Since a large section of tribals use liquor, it is a health hazard which can be a hurdle for their overall development in a globalised world. There should be effort on the part of NGOs and activists to create awareness to control the menace of liquor among the tribals.

Table 5.6

Health Status of Tribals in Kerala Ten Years Ago and at Present

Description	*Ten years ago*		*At present*	
	Number of Respondents	*%age*	*Number of Respondents*	*%age*
Utilisation of different types of health services by tribals				
Tribal treatment	219	27.4	13	1.6
Ayurveda	24	3.0	20	2.5
Allopathy	281	35.1	687	85.9
Homeopathy	2	0.3	2	0.4
Tribal treatment and allopathy	254	31.8	49	6.1
Ayurveda and allopathy	3	0.4	16	2.0
Allopathy and homeopathy	8	1.0	10	1.3
Tribal treatment, ayurveda and allopathy	9	1.1	—	—
Type of hospital normally tribals go to				
Not applicable	219	27.4	13	1.6
Primary health centre	8	1.0	45	5.6
Government hospital	512	64.0	469	58.6
Private hospital	23	2.9	125	15.6
Primary health centre and government hospital	3	0.4	6	0.8
Government and private hospitals	35	4.4	99	12.4
PHC, government and private hospitals	—	—	43	5.4
Availability of medical care for tribals in government hospitals				
No	328	41.0	433	54.1
Yes	253	31.6	354	44.3
Tribal treatment	219	27.4	13	1.6
Reasons for not getting medical care for tribals in government hospitals				
Those getting sufficient medical care	253	31.6	354	44.3
Tribal treatment	219	27.4	13	1.6
Lack of technical facilities	111	13.9	17	2.1
Non-availability of medicine	71	8.9	208	26.0
Unsatisfactory nursing care	6	0.8	18	2.3
Lack of technical facilities and Non-availability of medicine	97	12.1	95	11.9
Others	43	5.5	95	11.9

While inquiring about the types of treatment that are available to the tribals, it was surprising to note that a substantial proportion of the tribal respondents (86%) has got adapted to allopathy treatment compared to only 35 per cent ten years back.

At present the treatment of tribals from government hospitals is 58.7 per cent. On the other hand dependence on private hospitals has increased drastically over the years from 3 to 16 per cent, while dependence on government and private hospitals together increased from 4 to 12 per cent.

The major reasons for the tribals for not going to the government hospitals at present is non-availability of medicine (26%) while it was only 9 per cent ten years back. Other reasons for not going to the government hospitals at present are lack of technical facilities and non-availability of medicines together, in addition to unsatisfactory nursing care. If these three major reasons are added up together, they come to 40 per cent in contrast to 22 per cent ten years back. This means that 40 per cent of the tribals did not go to the government hospitals due to these reasons; instead they went to private hospitals for their health needs.

Data about a good health situation of tribals as revealed in the survey research are confirmed by the case studies. In all the three tribal villages including Marakadavu in Wayanad district where there was incidence of starvation death some years back, the health of the people was reported to be good. Still, there were some black spots. It was reported from Paliyakudy that there were more cases of illness now than earlier due to lack of nutritious food. They were not able to have sufficient food due to shortage of employment and income. Secondly, all three villages reported that traditional tribal medicine and treatment were fast disappearing except for curing small illnesses. At present most of the tribals in these villages go for allopathic treatment as the survey study also reveals. But in recent years they are going to private hospitals since the government hospitals on which they totally depended in the past, do not have enough medicines and necessary medical amenities. As the tribals do not have much income they struggle to find money for treatment in private hospitals. When they do so, it is at the expense of their basic needs like food and clothing. Those who cannot afford to pay private hospitals are deprived of good treatment and medicines, and thus their health is adversely affected.

The increased dependence of tribals on private hospitals at present compared to the situation ten years back, is to be read along with the main reasons they cited for not going to government hospitals, namely non-availability of medicines, technical facilities and nursing care at government hospitals. This is the experience of people of Kerala in general since they get prescription from the government hospitals but have to spend money outside for medicines and technical facilities.

Education of Tribal Children

Education is one of the vehicles that transmit culture to the new generation. Liberal education can also enrich and purify cultures. So it can be taken as part of culture. Existing studies show that there has not been lowering of educational level or standard of tribal children before the reform period in comparison with the post-reform period. Therefore, collection of data and their analysis are confined to the present situation. This section will briefly analyse the present system of education, its drawbacks, and the reasons for the high drop-out rate among tribal children.

Table 5.7

Educational Drop-outs of Tribal Children in Kerala

Number of tribal children per family who discontinued studies before completing 10th standard						
No of children in a family	Nil	1	2	3	4	5
Frequency	589	135	56	18	1	1
%	73.6	16.9	7	2.3	0.1	0.1

A major social problem among the tribals is their lack of education. Since their settlements are in remote areas and since their sociocultural background is different from that in urban areas, literacy level is generally low and drop-out rate is high. The average literacy level of respondents was 53 per cent, as seen in Table 3.1. Hence, the question about the dropouts among the children and reasons for the same was put to the respondents. Drop-out rate of children with one child per family was reported to be 17 per cent. A large number of children had dropped out from school before reaching tenth standard and 17 per cent of the respondents' households had at least one drop-out. In 7 per cent of the respondents' households there were two children as drop-outs. A higher rate of drop-outs from school with four or five from each family was also reported. Average drop-out rate till tenth standard was 39 per cent among tribal children in Kerala.

Table 5.8

Reasons for Drop-outs of Tribal Children from 1st to 10th Standard

	No. of Respondents	*Percentage*
Not applicable	589	73.6
Closing down government schools	5	0.6
Inability to get admission in private schools	4	0.5
High fee structure in private schools	18	2.3
Religious rituals restraining education	13	1.6
Absence of boarding schools	1	0.1
Discrimination of tribal children	1	0.1
Low standard of government schools	8	1.0
Others (specify)	12	1.5
Closing government schools and high fee structure of private schools	5	0.6
Religious rituals restraining education and low quality of government schools	19	2.4
Low standard of government school and financial difficulties	125	15.6

This table gives the reasons for the high drop-out rate among tribal children. A large proportion of the respondents (16%) reported a combined reason of low standard of government school and financial difficulties. Another combined reason was religious rituals restraining education and low quality of government schools (2%), which was followed by religious rituals restraining education (2%) and high fee structure in private schools (2%). Most of the tribal children study in government schools which are of poor quality, and tribal schools run by the government are abysmally low in standard without even basic facilities. The tribals are at the same time not able to go to private schools due to financial difficulties. This situation partly explains the reason for high drop-out rate among tribal children.

In the three tribal villages selected for case study, the drop-out rate in lower primary schools had decreased considerably since they were functioning in the village itself and since lumpsum grant and noon-meals are provided regularly. But it was very high in classes from five to ten in all villages. At Mully in Palakkad district, the drop-out rate of tribal children in these classes was 10–50 per cent. The reasons stated were many. Some of them were that children had to travel nearly 30 kilometres to reach the high school. Such a long distance is a disincentive for even non-tribal children, that too in remote areas without sufficient transport facilities. Secondly, lumpsum grant for tribal children was not distributed regularly at the time of re-opening of schools. This prevented them from buying text books which were too costly for tribals to buy from their own resources. Thirdly, language was also a problem for tribal children, since Malayalam is not their mother tongue.

Education is a must for the progress of any section of people in a globalised world. All the more so for tribals, the most backward community in the state of Kerela. Besides, since their livelihood through land and employment is already in jeopardy, education is the one opening for their socioeconomic development. Since the study shows low standard of school education among tribal children, urgent measures need to be taken for the advancement of quality education among them.

Status of Tribal Women in Kerala

Status of women in a society is indicative of its sense of justice and equality. It tells about the attitude of men towards women's position in family and society, share in property and wealth, and share in the decision-making process. In other words, gender sensitivity is part of the culture of a society. Therefore, women's position is considered part of the cultural aspect of tribal life, which traditionally gave a fairly good status to women. The study here considers the effect of globalisation on the status of tribal women in Kerala. This section looks at the socioeconomic situation of tribal women today, and compares the employment and wages of women ten years back and at present.

The following tables deal with the education, marital status, occupation, monthly income, social participation and saving pattern of tribal women.

Table 5.9

Proportion of Gender by Educational Status in Tribal Household

Educational Status	*Male*	*Female*
Illiterate	32.44	40.81
Drop-out	7.89	8.22
Literate	8.76	8.15
Primary education	18.80	16.03
Upper primary	14.58	11.04
High school	15.32	12.66
Plus2 or Pre degree	1.67	1.89
Degree	0.27	0.47
Postgraduation	0.07	0.34
Professional	0.13	0.00
Others	0.07	0.40

The educational level of the tribal men and women in Kerala shows that 32 per cent of men and 41 per cent of women are illiterate. Comparative analysis explains that the percentage of education for tribal boys at school level is higher than for girls, and the educational standard for boys in higher-levels too is higher than for girls. Literacy level of tribal women and educational standard of tribal girls are much lower than tribal men and boys respectively. This is in contrast to the situation of girls in Kerala where they are equal or even better than boys in educational standard. This means that tribal girls are not getting equal treatment in education. In a globalised world this will put them in a disadvantageous position.

Table 5.10

Proportion of Gender by Marital Status in Tribal Household in Kerala

Marital Status	*Male*	*Female*
Single	30.18	23.43
Married	67.02	63.70
Widow	0.00	9.57
Widower	2.30	0.00
Divorced	0.16	0.33
Separated	0.33	2.23
Unwedded mothers	0.00	0.74

The marital status of tribals shows that there are more male single persons (30%) than female single persons (23%). The percentages of married men and women are 67 per cent and 64 per cent respectively. There are more widows (10%) than widowers (2%) among tribals. The rate of separated women (2%) is higher than that of separated men (0.33%). Since there are more widows and separated women than men in these categories, they have to depend on the other family members for their life and livelihood. With decreasing number of working days especially for women, the situation of widows and separated women can be at a disadvantage.

Table 5.11

Proportion of Gender by Occupational Status in Tribal Household

Occupational Status	*Male*	*Female*
Unemployed	31.77	45.25
Coolie workers	48.63	38.38
Farmers	12.17	8.22
Technical workers	0.33	0.20
Clerks	0.07	0.00
Government employees	1.40	0.54
Collectors of forest produce	1.40	0.74
Petty business	0.27	0.00
Others	1.40	4.85
Coolie and farmers	2.14	1.75
Coolie and collectors of forest produce	0.40	0.07

Table 5.12

Proportion of Gender by Monthly Agricultural Income in Tribal Household

Amount of Income (in Rupees)	*Male*	*Female*
No income	84.82	96.23
Below 500	10.50	3.10
501–1,000	2.81	0.47
1,000–1,500	1.47	0.13
1,501 and above	0.40	0.07

The study excluded children below five years of age.

Table 5.13

Proportion of Gender by Monthly Non-Agricultural Income in Tribal Household

Amount of Income (in Rupees)	*Male*	*Female*
No income	43.81	57.10
Below 500	32.31	34.61
501–1000	20.54	6.73
1000–1500	1.61	1.01
1501–2000	0.33	0.07
2000 and above	1.40	0.47

The study excluded children below five years of age.

The sex-wise occupational distribution of tribals indicates that 32 per cent of men are unemployed while the corresponding figure for women is 46 per cent. In different segments of the occupation, females are significantly backward than males. About 96 per cent of females have no income from agriculture while only 3 per cent are getting income from agriculture (below 500 per month). Eleven per cent of males get income from the same source. While 44 per cent of tribal men do not have non-agricultural income, 57 per cent of tribal women do not have income. The data shows that more women are unemployed than men and that most of the women do not have any personal income. This implies that tribal women have lost their independence and status which they had in earlier times to manage the affairs of the family. This is indirectly connected to globalisation as is seen in the annual working days of tribal women.

Table 5.14

Proportion of Gender by Social Participation in Tribal Household in Kerala

Type of Social Participation	*Male*	*Female*
Nil	77.06	71.18
Political parties	12.31	6.60
Arts and sports club	1.74	0.47
Cooperative society	2.41	0.40
Mahila Samaj	0.07	0.13
Self-help groups	1.87	3.30
Kudumbashree	2.47	12.46
Others	0.80	0.40
Cooperative society and Kudumbashree	0.67	0.61
Self-help groups and Kudumbashree	0.60	4.44

The study excluded children below five years of age.

With regard to social participation, more men (78%) do not have social participation than women (71%). Participation in political parties is much higher percentage (12%) for men than for women (7%), while in 'Kudumbashree' women perform far better (12%) than men (2%). This shows that women find SHGs and 'Kudumbashree' more relevant than men, especially since they are primarily meant for women. This fact indicates that for greater social participation tribal women should be encouraged to participate in SHGs. The lower percentage of women in social participation, particularly in political parties, indicates less involvement of women in wider political and social processes and decision making. This again can be connected to the cultural situation of the tribals in which women are not getting opportunities to be involved in the wider society.

Table 5.15

Proportion of Gender by Saving Pattern of Tribal Household

Type of saving pattern	*Male*	*Female*
Nil	92.34	81.35
Chits/Funds	0.20	0.20
Co-operative society	0.33	0.13
Post office savings	0.27	0.40
Bank deposits	0.67	0.27
Self-help groups	2.53	6.94
Kudumbashree	2.27	10.30
Others	1.40	0.40

In saving pattern too, a similar male-female proportion is found in the study. While 92 per cent of tribal men do not have any saving, the corresponding figure for women is 81 per cent. This higher saving rate for women is shown to be due to SHGs and 'Kudumbashree'. While 10 per cent of tribal women have saving in 'Kudumbashree', only 2 per cent of men have saving in the same. In SHGs also a much higher percentage of women have saving than men (7% and 3% respectively). These data also reveal that SHGs could be one way of encouraging tribals to develop saving habit.

The status of women in three villages selected for case study is not encouraging. Their position had lowered together with the decline of tribal structure and culture. It was reported from all three villages that workload of women had increased in recent years since they work both inside and outside the house. However, they are not as economically independent as they used to be, since they do not get enough work and since they do not get equal pay as men get for the same work. They have to travel long to collect firewood as forests are destroyed and forest produce is not much available. In hilly areas they have a hard time collecting water. There is sexual exploitation of women by outsiders. At Marakadavu village in Wayanad district at least four cases of unwed mothers were reported. But at Paliyakudy village, which is close to Thekkady, a national tourist centre with a Wild Life Sanctuary, there was not a single case of sexual exploitation. The reasons, as they themselves said, were that people were vigilant and women's organisations took up such issues. Besides, unlike in the other villages mentioned above, women were active participants in socioeconomic organisations of Panchayat and NGOs. Their experience shows that for greater role and status for women, they should be encouraged to form and join organisations like Self-Help Groups and Mahila Samajams.

In the last chapter the study showed that agricultural work, the main source of livelihood for tribals in Kerala, had declined considerably in the post-reform period compared to the pre-reform period. In this section, comparison was also made between the employment available to tribal men and women (Table 4.5). It was found that the average annual working days for women was 99 during pre-reform period while for men it was 135 during the same period. At present the average working days for women is 45, while it is 72 for men during the same period. Here again though, for both men and women the annual working days had been drastically reduced from the pre-reform period, than men in the rate of decrease was much greater for women (more than half). Besides, having just 45 days of work a year means that it is not a real source of livelihood. When women are not able to earn income the tribal family as a whole suffers since women have greater responsibility to provide food and other essential commodities for the family. Therefore, decrease in employment of women affects not only the family but also the independence and dignity of tribal women. As was shown in the earlier chapter, the decrease in annual working days of women was due to less agricultural operations in plantations like coffee and tea where tribal women were employed. Agricultural operations had been reduced or dropped fully in some cases because agriculture was not remunerative mainly due to crash in prices of cash crops. Thus the rate of decrease in annual working days was higher for women than for men and so tribal women's life was worse affected than men's.

Agricultural wage for tribals not only did not rise in actual terms during the post-reform period, but in certain places it was even reduced (Table 4.5). Though both tribal men and women were affected by low wage in the post-reform period the tribal women were more affected than men. The reason was that the tribal women had a higher rate of decrease in the number of working days and had a much lower wage than men.

Social and Political Participation of Tribals in Kerala

In a democratic country the level of political awareness and participation in public affairs is a necessary means of socioeconomic progress of its citizens, especially the marginalised. Therefore, the study has enquired into the level of participation of tribals in sociopolitical organisations

Table 5.16

Participation of Tribals in Sociopolitical Organisations

Description	*Number of Respondents*	*Percentage*
Types of social participation by the tribals		
Nil	486	60.8
Political parties	121	15.1
Arts and sports club	11	1.4
Cooperative society	35	4.4
Mahila Samaj	2	0.3
Self-help groups	28	3.5
Kudumbashree	80	10.0
Cooperative society and Kudumbashree	8	1.0
Self-help groups and Kudumbashree	26	3.3
Others	3	0.4
Total	800	100
The willingness of tribals to join in SHG/Kudumbashree in future		
No	362	45.3
Yes	330	41.3

Cont'd...

Cont'd...

Not applicable	108	13.4
Total	800	100
Participation of tribals in Gram Sabha meetings		
No	161	20.1
Yes	639	79.9
Total	800	100
Participation of tribals in "Oorukootam"		
No	368	46.0
Yes	432	54.0
Total	800	100
Participation of tribals in tribal organisations		
No	449	56.1
Yes	351	43.9
Total	800	100
Willingness of tribals to participate in tribal organisations in future		
No	122	15.3
Yes	327	40.9
Tribals who participate at present	351	43.9
Total	800	100
Participation of tribals in tribal agitations		
No	531	66.4
Yes	269	33.6
Total	800	100
Willingness of tribals to participate in tribal agitation in future		
No	120	15.0
Yes	411	51.4
Tribals who participate at present	269	33.6
Total	800	100
Willingness of tribals to solve the problems of tribal community through collective action in future		
No	78	9.8
Yes	722	90.3
Total	800	100

Cont'd...

Cont'd...

Types of organisations with whom tribals are willing to cooperate for collective action in future		
Not ready for collective action	78	9.8
Each tribal group separately	47	5.9
All tribal groups together	504	63.0
Through non-party political organisations	33	4.1
Through political parties	17	2.1
All tribal groups together and Non-political activities	121	15.2
Total	800	100

The respondents were asked whether they participated in some sociopolitical activity. It was observed that the vast majority of tribals was not involved in any kind of social activity (61%). Among the respondents who had some kind of social participation (39%), 15 per cent were involved in political parties, followed by those participating in other social groups called 'Kudumbashree', the self-help groups organised by Panchayats (10%). Four per cent of the members were in cooperative societies while another 4 per cent were in self-help groups (SHGs). Yet 3 per cent were active in both SHGs and 'Kudumbashree'. Since the SHGs and 'Kudumbashree' are grass-root level social groups, the respondents who were not involved in their activities were again asked about their willingness to join such groups in future. Forty-seven per cent of the respondents expressed their willingness to join such social groups in future.

To know about the respondents' involvement in the grass-roots level politics, that is local self-government such as village Gram Sabha and village Panchayat, a question was asked whether they participated in Gram Sabha meetings in their area. It was reported that a substantial proportion of the respondents attended the meetings (80%). Similarly, among the tribal communities there is another local meeting called 'Oorukootam' (traditional meetings of tribals), and 54 per cent of the respondents stated to be attending those meetings. Tribals could be further encouraged to participate in Panchayat level meetings. For this, they could be motivated about Panchayati Raj and other grass-root level organisations through seminars and training programmes.

The findings of the study about sociopolitical participation are confirmed by the experience of the three villages selected for case study. Tribals in these villages also are not active workers of political parties, though many of them believe in the ideology of either the Congress or the Marxist party. Most of the people in all the three villages participate regularly in Grama Sabha meetings. In fact, at Paliyakudy in Idduki district everybody attended these meetings, though not all were active participants. Whenever 'Oorukootam' was called by the Panchayat they participated. This shows that Panchayati Raj was successful and effective with tribals especially under the People's Plan Campaign. The reasons could be that they got many benefits like houses and drinking water, and that Panchayat was localised to their situation. Panchayati Raj, as local self-government, could be an agent which can be of benefit to the tribals. Therefore, for active and meaningful participation in Grama Sabha, the tribals should be systematically trained in Panchayati Raj.

The respondents were also asked about their participation in any of the tribal organisations. It was identified that only 44 per cent of the tribals had participated in the activities of their tribal organisations/associations. The respondents who had not participated in the activities of tribal organisation were asked whether they were willing to join such organisations in future. A vast majority of the respondents (84%) replied that they were ready to join such organisations.

A question was put to the tribal respondents about their willingness to solve the problems of their community. The actual question was whether they had participated in any of the tribal agitations. It was reported that only 34 per cent of the respondents had participated in some form of tribal agitation at the local or state level. The respondents who had not participated in any such tribal agitation were again asked whether they were ready to participate in such agitations in future. A notably great proportion of them (85%) replied that they were ready to participate in such agitations.

To check the collective strength and cooperation among them, the tribals were asked whether they were ready to solve the problems of their community through collective action. Most of the respondents (90%) stated that they were ready to solve the problems of tribal community through collective action. Among them, 63 per cent said that they would like it to be done by all tribal groups together while 7 per cent were for collective action by each tribal group separately. Only a small per cent of respondents stated they were ready to work with political parties (3%).

A vast majority of the tribals expressed their willingness to join agitations for the cause of tribals in Kerala. This is a positive information for organisers of state-level tribal movements and it also shows that there is awareness among the tribals about organising and agitating to get their rights. A state-level organisation should exploit this positive attitude of the Adivasis. Going with the above description is the opinion of 90 per cent of the tribals that they are willing to work collectively as Adivasis for the Adivasi cause. Out of this group 63 per cent mentioned they were for all tribal organisations coming to work collectively at the state-level. Further, it is significant to note that only 2 per cent of tribals wanted collective action through political parties. It means that most tribals are willing to work under non-party political organisations not affiliated to any political party.

This chapter presented data about the impact of globalisation on the sociocultural life of the tribals. This aspect consisted of the cultural and religious practices of tribals, their health, education, tribal women's situation, and participation of tribals in sociopolitical organisations. The following chapter will analyse these data and the data on livelihood to examine the overall impact of globalisation on the life of the tribals in Kerala.

6

Analysis of the Impact of Globalisation on the Tribals

Adivasis are the most backward section of the population in India, who are facing a lot of problems all over the country, particularly in Kerala. In this state their live issues have come to the limelight along with their longstanding struggle for land. Since their employment opportunities are decreasing their means of livelihood are affected and their education, health and food security are being threatened. This study tried to examine how globalisation has affected the tribals in Kerala. Both primary and secondary data were used for this purpose. Primary data was collected using survey method, case studies of three tribal villages in three districts, and personal unstructured interviews.

The data collected from these primary sources were presented in the previous chapters. This chapter will analyse these data, which will be complimented by secondary data. The analysis is to study the overall impact of globalisation on the livelihood and sociocultural life of the tribals in Kerala. Before this is done, responses of the tribals to two other questions and their analysis are given. The first question tried to find out whether the tribals had any benefit from globalisation and the second one was to give suggestions to solve the problems the tribals are facing due to the policies of globalisation. Therefore, the analysis of data will include the opinions of tribals regarding the benefit they have received through globalisation policies of the government and their suggestions to solve the problems supposed to have been caused by globalisation like its impact on their livelihood, on their cultural and religious practices, on health, education, and on tribal women. Each section will analyse the findings from the study with the support of secondary data.

The objective of the study was to find out how globalisation has affected the life of the tribals in Kerala. A survey method was used to enquire from the tribals the effect of globalisation on their life. As part of the survey, the tribals were asked about the benefits they received from the policies and programmes of the government during the last ten years viz. the period of globalisation. This question was aimed at an objective evaluation of globalisation with its positive and negative impact on the tribals.

Table 6.1

Benefits Received from the Policies and Programmes of the Government During the Last Ten Years

Description	*Number of Respondents*	*Percentage*
Nil	355	44.4
Free ration	3	0.4
Housing	254	31.8
Housing and free ration	23	2.9
Housing and electricity	20	2.5
Housing and latrine	4	0.5
Housing and road	7	0.9
Electricity and drinking water	2	0.3
Housing, road and electricity	30	3.8
Solar lamp, free ration and fertilizer	91	11.4
Housing and solar lamps	11	1.4
Total	800	100

As is shown in the table, majority of respondents (55.6%) reported that they were recipients of some kind of government benefits. Among those who got some government benefits, a majority (32%) received housing benefits. This is followed by a sizeable section (11%) of tribals who got solar light, free ration and fertilizer together.

The study reveals that majority of the tribals received some benefit or other from the government in the last ten years. The benefits they received included housing, solar light, free ration, roads, electricity and drinking water. That the government programmes have benefited the tribals, the most marginalised group in Kerala, is positive and encouraging. But it is to be remembered that these programmes existed much before the ten year period of globalisation. Significantly none of them have mentioned any benefits connected with globalisation like information technology and cell phones. This means that the real benefits of globalisation have not touched the lives of tribals. Reports from case studies and interviews also confirm this factor.

The tribal respondents were also asked to give their own suggestions to solve the problems faced by the tribals in connection with globalisation e.g., the new policies of the government on privatisation and liberal import.

Table 6.2

Suggestions to Solve the Problems the Tribals Face due to Policies of the Government like Privatisation and Liberalisation

Description	*Number of Respondents*	*Percentage*
No suggestions	583	72.9
Distribution of promised land	59	7.4
Increase in the price of agricultural products	62	7.8
Use of Swadeshi products	8	1.0
Decrease in the price of ration items	7	0.9
Protest against the high price of food items	67	8.4
Change in the import policy	6	0.8
Change in the tribal policy of the government	1	1
Government should change the new economic policies	6	0.8
Others	1	0.1
Total	800	100

We found that a notably large proportion of the tribal respondents could not give any suggestion regarding this question (73%). Among those who offered some suggestions, 8 per cent wanted to oppose the high price of food items, another 8 per cent demanded increase in the price of agricultural products and 7 per cent wanted distribution of land promised to them by the government. Other suggestions given by a few included use of local products ("swadeshi" goods), reduction in the price of civil supply items, a change in the export and import policy, and a change in the present economic reforms.

It is understandable that most of the tribal respondents were not in a position to answer the question as to how to solve the problems arising from globalisation, since it is a technical question. At the same time the responses of the minority who answered this question are revealing, since they seem to have understood the implications of globalisation. The highest percentage of tribals wanted the price of food items to be reduced. If the answers of other respondents are taken into account it could mean they were referring to prices of essential commodities distributed through the Public Distribution System (PDS). As will be shown later, the government had increased the price of these food items, and the tribals were not able to pay the new prices. The respondents may also have meant prices of goods sold in the open market as they have to buy them for their survival. This can also include goods manufactured and sold by private companies as well as government companies. As the government decreases its subsidy to essential goods and services, price of these goes on increasing. The message from the tribals seems to be that subsidies given to essential commodities should be continued and that government should not withdraw from areas connected with the basic needs of the poor. The next highest group of respondents suggested increase in the price of agricultural products. This can mean that they understood the connection between the decrease in their price and the liberalisation policy of the government. They implied that imports should be curbed and support price should be given to agriculture so that the farmers get a remunerative price. This is corroborated by the suggestion of others to change the import-export policy of the government, which is directly linked to the policy of liberalisation. If there is adequate price for farm products, Adivasis who have land and cultivation can benefit. Those who do not have land also can benefit as the farmers will restart agricultural operations which will give employment to the tribals who are mostly dependent on the agricultural sector. A small percentage of respondents were for "Swadeshi goods". This could mean that they were against flooding the market with foreign goods often imported from other countries, which are beneficial mainly to the rich and middle-class and not to the marginalised groups like the tribals. This is also connected with the above-mentioned suggestion to change import-export policy of the government. A significant suggestion by a small proportion of respondents was that the present economic system should be changed, meaning that the globalisation policy of the government should be reverted. This can mean that they are dissatisfied with the globalisation process which has made their life very miserable. A quarter of the respondents suggested that the government should distribute land which it had promised to the tribals. This means that they are conscious of their right to land.

The villages of Mulli and Marakadavu, two out of the three villages selected for case study, do not find any hope for Adivasis in the future. They assert that the government has destroyed their life, livelihood and culture totally, especially with its policy of globalisation. The politicians and the government officials steal all the funds meant for tribal development. Tribals will gradually die of illness and starvation, and their very survival is in peril. The tribal respondents at Marakadavu feel that they can survive if they get land for cultivation. They will have to organise themselves and work jointly for this, since real liberation is possible only through the tribals themselves.

In contrast, the tribals of Paliyakudy in Idukky district, the third village included in the case study, believe that the Adivasis have a future if they get education at all levels. Information technology, if made available to the tribals, will help in their development. The other two villages were skeptical about the relevance of information technology for tribals. They said, "What is the use of information technology for those of us who are illiterate? We cannot even dream of it since it involves a huge expense."

Analysis of the Impact of Globalisation on the Livelihood of the Tribals in Kerala

It is interesting to note that none of the tribals interviewed mentioned any benefit of globalisation for tribals. Tribal respondents in the survey study and case study also did not mention any merits of globalisation for tribals. The data regarding the negative effects of globalisation as revealed in the study are analysed below. This section on livelihood will include land, employment, wage and availability of essential commodities.

Land and Cultivation

The study shows that 59 per cent of the tribals do not have land at all. A great percentage (45%) has less than one acre of land. Case studies of the three villages, Paliyakudy in Idukky district, Mully in Palakkad district and Marakadavu in Wayanad district confirm these findings of the survey. Though more than half of the people of these villages have land, it is less than 50 cents mostly owned by joint families. The study confirms the reality of the tribals in the state where a good percentage does not have land. Even when they have a bit of land it is not a real source of income and so they have to go for wage labour. The tribals lost their land over the last many years, though only 1 per cent lost land during the last ten years of the globalisation period. Land is not only a source of livelihood but also a symbol of sociocultural life for the tribals everywhere. Naturally providing land for the future existence of tribals is a must, and it is mainly for land that the tribals have been agitating but have not yet got it.

Among those who have land, 28 per cent were practicising subsistence farming ten years back while at present those following subsistence farming have been reduced to 13 per cent. In its place those having commercial farming increased to 22 per cent from 3 per cent ten years back. This means commercialisation of subsistence economy is increasingly taking place in Kerala within the globalisation period. This is a reflection of the increasing tendency of cultivation of cash crops in the state as a whole. But it has its disadvantages. First of all, tribals who have a bit of land are affected by the decrease in price of cash crops due to globalisation. Secondly, when the price of cash crops like pepper and coffee crashed, the tribals lost not only the only means of income but also the food crops on which they could survive. That is why the question whether the tribals with a little land should go in for commercial crops or should be encouraged to cultivate food crops, becomes very relevant. If they cultivate food crops they can survive on them irrespective of fluctuations in price of cash crops. In short, distribution of land to the tribals is very basic to their welfare, which can be ensured only with the assistance and encouragement of the government.

Tribal Forest Bill

The Scheduled Tribes and other Traditional Forest Dwellers' Recognition of Forest Rights Act, 2006 was passed by the Parliament in 2006 and has become a law throughout the country. This law gives certain rights and privileges connected with forests to the tribals. Since tribal land and life are very much related to forest it is pertinent to see some of the advantageous provisions of this law for the tribals:

1. The law gives rights to the forest dwelling scheduled tribals to hold and live on forest land and to cultivate it for livelihood.
2. The tribals are given rights to collect minor forest produce as a means of livelihood.
3. Rights of settlement and ownership of traditionally owned forest villages by tribals can be converted into revenue villages.
4. If forest land occupied by tribals is taken away for common purposes, they will have right to full rehabilitation with alternative land.
5. Grama Sabha of the area can decide on the rights of tribals over forest land where they are living, and determine the nature of resettlement and rehabilitation of tribals evicted for common purposes.

Since the Tribal Forest Act is about rights and occupation of forest land by tribals, it is relevant for the tribals in Kerala also. The tribals who are living within the area of reserved forest or close to it as in Idukky or Palakkad district, could be given forest rights and title deed so that they are not evicted on the basis of forest laws, and are also able to get the benefit of electricity and other public utilities. Secondly, tribals are allowed to collect minor forest produce as permitted by the Act so that they have supplementary income for survival. Thirdly, tribals are to be properly resettled and rehabilitated in case of eviction for common purposes. The central and state governments should make necessary rules and legal structures to implement the provisions of this Act so that the tribals in Kerala get all the benefits of this Act at the earliest. Tribal organisations and NGOs working among tribals can facilitate in getting this long awaited law operationalised in the state.

Impact of Globalisation on the Employment and Income of the Tribals

It was the availability of employment of tribals, which was most directly affected by globalisation. According to the survey 29 per cent of men have only 50–100 days of work, while the figure was 5 per cent ten years back. While 34 per cent had up to 300 days of work a year ten years back, only 3 per cent of tribals have that much at present. Among women, 31 per cent had 100–200 days of work a year ten years back while only 11 per cent have that many days at present. While 16 per cent of women had 200–300 days of work ten years ago their percentage had dwindled to 2 per cent today. If we take into account the fact that 21 per cent of men and 29 per cent of women do not have any work, we can gauge the pathetic situation of tribals in Kerala. The drastic decrease in the number of working days has made the tribals more miserable during the period of globalisation. This is confirmed by the rate of working days for the tribals in the villages chosen for case studies. At Marakkadavu in Wayanad district, the average working days for men was 100–120 days while earlier they were getting 250–300 days of work. In Mully village of Palakkad district, 100 tribals worked in the nearby tea estate ten years ago, while at present only ten get work there. This is because there are no agricultural operations in the tea estate due to fall in price of tea. Some tribal youth were getting jobs in textile mills in Coimbatore, Tamil Nadu but they had lost them since many of these factories had closed down rendering thousands jobless. This is apparently due to globalisation since the traditional small scale factories were not getting the support and subsidies during the pre-reform period that they used to get. We can also notice the much lower number of working days a year for tribal women than for men. This reveals the poor economic situation of tribal women.

The daily wage for 39 per cent of men was Rs 51–100 ten years back, while only 1 per cent receives that much wage at present. Only 0.4 per cent of women get the same range of wage now compared to 4 per cent ten years back. While 45 per cent of women got Rs 26–50 as wage ten years back, at present only 25 per cent receive that much. In the matter of wage also tribal women were discriminated against and had greater misery. The average daily wage for men and women at present is Rs 68 and Rs 40 respectively. Though there was no decrease in the wages of tribals there was no increase either. The villages selected for case study also did not report any decrease in wage during the last ten years. Since the price of essential commodities had increased considerably during the last few years, the tribals got less quality of life with the same money than in the previous years. This is all the more so since the number of working days has come down drastically. Thus the wage of the tribals was adversely affected during the period of globalisation.

The data from the survey and case studies reveal that the average working days per year for the tribals had decreased drastically both for men and women. The reason cited by the respondents themselves is the crash in prices of practically all the cash crops, especially coffee, tea and pepper. Fall in prices of cash crops was attributed by the respondents to the import of the same products from other countries during the post-reform period. Import of these agricultural products was mainly due to the reduced rate of excise and import duty on these products. In the post-reform period this is related to the liberalisation policy of the government based on the regulations of the World Trade Organisation. According to the policy of the government, it had to lower the tariff for imports and allow import of many goods liberally. Thus coffee and tea from other countries especially Sri Lanka were imported to India at a much cheaper rate than that of Indian products, resulting in drastic fall in the price of these commodities. This happened during the last ten years when the government vigorously implemented the policies of globalisation.

When the price of cash crops fell below the remunerative price, the farmers either stopped or drastically reduced agricultural operations for these crops, especially coffee and tea. Since the tribals were dependent on these farms and estates for wage labour, they lost their regular employment there. Thus the average working days of the tribals per year decreased as was shown in our study, resulting in less income, leading to adverse effect on their livelihood. Thus the policies of globalisation followed by the Indian government directly impacted on the livelihood of the tribals, the most marginalised group in India and Kerala, and made their life more vulnerable than earlier.

Almost all those who were interviewed personally asserted that there was decrease in job opportunities for tribals as a result of globalisation. "Adivasis face the greatest threat from shortage of employment which is related to the policy of globalisation", said one tribal woman leader. In the words of another one who was interviewed, "as a result of globalisation the Adivasis face unemployment, poverty, disease, starvation and death. They are on the verge of extinction." Another remarked, "Adivasis are the first victims of globalisation." Thus according to the respondents of personal interviews globalisation has caused poverty and misery for tribals in Kerala.

Adivasis who have some land are also adversely affected since they do not get remunerative price for their cash crops. Thus income from their land, which is often less than one acre, is also considerably reduced. Since tribals totally depend on agriculture or agriculture-related occupation, their livelihood is seriously affected. As one tribal said, "When there is no cultivation due to crash in price of agricultural products we are badly hit". This is all the more so since their traditional sources of livelihood like forest produce and cottage industry are not existing now. "The crisis in agriculture which has come as part of globalisation has affected the tribals most", said one social activist.

The survey study revealed that the number of working days for tribals during the last ten years of globalisation has considerably decreased. The villages selected for case study also confirmed the decrease of working days for tribals. Thus decrease in employment of tribals during the post-reform period is a fact identified and confirmed by the survey, case study and interviews. So the most glaring effect of globalisation on tribals in Kerala is the reduction in their working days leading to deprivation of their source of livelihood.

Globalisation and Agriculture in India

From the survey study, personal interviews and case studies it was seen how most of the tribals in Kerala lost their land, their most important source of livelihood. When they lost their land, the only means of livelihood available to them was wage labour. Thus most of them started working in plantations of cash crops and paddy fields as coolie workers. When the price of agricultural products drastically came down, farming operations got reduced, resulting in decrease in employment. The Adivasis who were depending on agriculture were thus badly affected. The study showed how the employment available per year for the Adivasis decreased, and thus their economic well-being was affected. Globalisation appears to be the main reason for the crisis in agriculture in India, particularly in Kerala. If there is a drastic fall in employment in the agricultural sector, how is it related to the liberalisation policy of the government regarding agriculture? This section examines whether globalisation has affected agriculture in India and in Kerala in order to see its impact on the tribals in Kerala.

Studies show that during the period of globalisation from 1991 onwards agriculture in India was facing a crisis in production and profits for the farmers and there was an overall decline in agricultural growth. The status report of the agricultural ministry says that the annual average farm growth rate has declined from 4.9 per cent in the eighth plan to 1.3 per cent in the tenth plan. The share of agriculture investment in Gross Domestic Product (GDP) declined from 1.99 per cent to 1.66 per cent during the same period (Parsai, 2006). The period referred to is the period during which the policy of globalisation through structural adjustment was implemented. This is explained by the pattern of the production of agricultural crops during the last five years.

Table 6.3

Agricultural Growth in India

	1998–1999	*1999–2000*	*2000–2001*
Food Production (in crores of tonnes)	20.35	20.89	19.90
Change from previous year (%)	5.8	2.7	– 4.7
Rate of agriculture growth (%)	178.0	176.8	170.6
Change from previous year (%)	7.7	– 0.7	– 3.5

Source: Economic Survey 2000–2001 (Kunjikannan, 2001: 30).

The table shows that the average growth of crop index fell from 5.8 per cent during 1998–99 to –4.7 per cent during 2000–01. This was due to the fall in investment in irrigation projects, which subsequently affected the productivity of small and marginal farmers (Franco, 2002: 9). To a certain extent, the drastic fall in growth rate can be explained by the drastic reduction in the investment in agriculture. Other indicators in agriculture explain it further. "The annual growth rate of food grain yield declined from 16 per cent in 1991–96 to 2.9 per cent in 2001–05" (Franco, 2002: 9). This is the period in which the policy of liberalisation was implemented. The area under cultivation declined from 128 million hectares in 1981–86 to 120–125 million hectares in 2001–2005 (Franco, 2002: 9). May be due to the fact of decline in growth rate of food grain and its area of cultivation, 27 per cent of farmers surveyed found farming unviable (Franco, 2002: 9). As a result of these developments the number of cultivators declined from 110.70 million in 1991 to 103.63 million in 2001 (Pawar, 2005). It was also pointed out that more than 20 per cent of farmers were below poverty line in India in 1999–2000 (Pawar, 2005). No wonder M.S. Swaminathan, Chairman of the National Commission on Agriculture said, "Indian agriculture is in a state of serious crisis. The rate of growth in food production has fallen below the population growth rate" (Swaminathan, 2005).

The impact of crisis in agriculture was seen by the increasing suicide rate among farmers, of which the highest rate was in Rajasthan—about 2000 suicides in three years of 2000–2002, and 500 in 2001 alone (*Deccan Herald*, 2002). The reasons reported were agriculture and animal husbandry recurring losses resulting in mounting debt burdens, economic reforms, rising cost of agriculture, denial of minimum support price, drought and debt burden (*Deccan Herald*, 2002). Thus among the several reasons for farmers' suicide, one is the economic reforms that were a part of globalisation. "Their tale of woe began in 1990s when India took its first step to liberalise, and worsened progressively from 1995" (*Deccan Herald*, 2002). The farmers' suicide in Andhra Pradesh, Karnataka, Maharashtra and Kerala indicates the desperate situation of farmers due to the crisis in agriculture. According to Chalam, "The first victim of the new economic policy appears to be the agricultural sector. The subsidies of the sector have been withdrawn and prices of most of the inputs have been raised" (Chalam, 1994: 37).

Thus we find from authoritative sources that agricultural growth declined drastically in the 1990s with the decrease in area of cultivation and in the number of cultivators in the farm section. This created a real crisis in agriculture, and a concrete expression of this crisis was the increasing number of suicide cases in a number of states in India. The reason for this crisis was a declining trend in investment in agriculture in the form of irrigation, subsidies etc. This phenomenon was part of the government's policy of reducing subsidies and withdrawal of government support to agriculture, which was a part of its policy of liberalisation and globalisation based on regulations of WTO and World Bank. Reduction in subsidy to agriculture was an important regulation of WTO enforced in most of the countries. Thus the crisis in agriculture due to decline in production and investment was found to be caused by the policy of globalisation followed by the government.

Globalisation and Agriculture in Kerala

If there was a crisis in agriculture throughout India as a result of globalisation, it was particularly so in Kerala with its over-dominance of cash crops. Special reasons related to cash crops have aggravated the problems in Kerala, which will be analysed in this section.

Cultivable land in Kerala got reduced from 5.03 lakh acres in 1994–95 to 3.36 lakhs in 2001 (*Mathrubhumi*, 2003). The price of practically all the major cash crops in Kerala crashed to an unprofitable level during this period. "The major tea and other plantations have been shut down throwing thousands out of work in the past two years" (Sainath, 2004). Because it was not profitable to cultivate tea, many tea estates were closed down in Wayanad and Idukky, the major tea producing districts. Many coffee estates in Wayanad also stopped agricultural operations. This resulted in massive loss of job for thousands of labourers, mostly tribals and Dalits. As one farmer from Wayanad put it, "the wages are down, pepper, coffee and everything is down. Only debt burden is up" (Sainath, 2004).

The impact of globalisation on cash crops like tea and coffee in Kerala was enormous. In Peerumedu taluk of Idukki district, an important taluk for tea, 50 per cent of the estates are in crisis with the owners leaving the estates or declaring lockout. Price of one kilogram of tea that fetched Rs 14 in 1996–97 got reduced to Rs 3 in 2000 (*Mathrubhumi*, 2003). Due to slash in price the estates got paralysed. Out of 36 estates in the taluk 22 got closed down and About 40,000 workers went out of job. Water, electricity, health care, education, accommodation and other benefits which were due to them as estate workers were no more available to them. So they were facing starvation and poverty (Sreedevi, 2003). "In Peerumedu, poverty is writ large on faces here. Malnourished women, near naked children, disillusioned men, all stand for that ugly reality" (Sreedevi, 2003: 2).

Tea industry is very important for Kerala and for the Indian economy. Kerala produced 10 per cent of the national output, in 2000–01 and 34 per cent of tea produced in South India. It is spread in 37,000 hectares of land, which is 8 per cent of the total area of cultivation in the country. Around 84,000 workers are employed in this industry (Sreedevi, 2003: 2). One of the main reasons for the crisis in tea industry was the fall in price due to import of cheap tea from Sri Lanka, which was on account of the liberalisation policy of government (Sreedevi, 2003: 2; *Mathrubhumi*, 2003). Cash crops like tea and coffee were liberally imported to India since tariffs and import duties on these products were drastically reduced as part of the liberalisation policy of the government. Free flow of goods among countries with low import duties was a requirement of the globalisation process. Therefore, crisis in agriculture in India, particularly in Kerala, is due to globalisation specifically enunciated by WTO and GATT.

As many as 64 per cent of the farmer households in Kerala were in debts in 2005 compared to the national average of 49 per cent, according to National Sample Survey Organisation (NSSO, 2003). The debt amount of farmers in the state stood second in the entire country. The total outstanding loan per household amounted to Rs 33,907, while the national average was Rs 12,585 (Cithare, 2005). The consequences of the agricultural crisis was the debt trap of farmers about which the above data speak. Farmers committed suicide in large numbers due to unrepayable loan. Over 600 farmers committed suicide between 2001 and 2005 in Kerala (Varghese, 2005: 4).

According to a statement by Chief Minister, A.K. Antony in 2003 in the Legislative Assembly, the number of suicide cases in Kerala increased from 17,048 in 1996–97 to 19,774 in 2000–02, which corresponds to the period of globalisation in India. The suicide rate went up from 15 per 1,000 population in 1997 to 27 per 1,000 in 2003 (*Deccan Herald*, 2003). The reason given by the State Commission for Women is globalisation. Kerala is "at the receiving end of adverse effects of globalisation, commercialisation and privatisation" (*Deccan Herald*, 2003). In other words the economic crisis triggered by globalisation is one of the major causes of suicide in Kerala.

Crisis in Agriculture and World Trade Organisation

"WTO and GATT agreement have very complex conditions and laws. Agricultural agreement and intellectual property rights implemented as part of these, has created very adverse impact on Indian agriculture" (Varghese, 2003). The price of coconut, pepper, ginger, tea, nutmeg etc. fell due to the agreement of the Central Government with countries like Sri Lanka, Indonesia and Malaysia. These countries were allowed to import these products duty free. This was admitted by the Central Agricultural Minister, Ajit Singh, when he said that Kerala was the most badly affected state in India, especially since Kerala depended on crash crops the price of which crashed due to WTO and globalisation (*Mathrubhumi*, 2002). Due to the import policy of the Central Government the price of major cash crops—coconut, rubber, pepper, coffee, tea, arecanut, ginger, cardamom, turmeric—fell steeply in the years 2000–2002. The agricultural sector in the state thus incurred a loss of Rs 6645 crores (Kerala Government, 2003). "Drought and disease hurt us. But it is free trade policies that have driven prices down" said a farmer from Wayanad (Sainath, 2004).

The price decline of major cash crops in Kerala due to the import policy of the government during 1995–2003, the post-reform period, is given below:

Table 6.4
Average Price Rate of Major Cash Crops in Kerala (Rs/quintal)

Crops	*Year*		
	1995	*1999*	*2003 (till Nov.)*
Dressed Coconut (1000)	3,104	4,933	4,601
Rubber (RSS-4)	5,204	3,148	4,770
Pepper	7,411	19,055	7,375
Cardamom	24,800	57,700	27,000
Ginger	6,169	6,776	5,066
Arecanut	5,410	10,411	4,017
Coffee	9,000	6,800	2,300
Tea	4,100	6,200	4,950

Source: State Agricultural Crop Price Fixing Board, Eco-state Department.

Except coconut all other crops faced a fall in price. Thus we find that globalisation has adversely affected agriculture in Kerala more than in any other state. That most of these crops are grown in the three districts we have chosen for study and where Adivasis depend on these crops for their livelihood, is again telling on their plight due to liberalisation. Due to lack of education and other reasons, Adivasis in Kerala did not have skills to take advantage of globalisation. Rather they suffered from deprivation since the employment opportunities decreased for them due to the crisis in agriculture, that was an offshoot of globalisation.

Globalisation and Adivasis in Kerala

The National Sample Survey (2003) states that one in two Adivasis lives below poverty line in rural India, which is almost double the figure for the general population in rural India. "What is worse, the only social category whose below-the-poverty line population increased in the 1990s, is the Adivasis". "In terms of changes in poverty in the 1990s, it is found that while scheduled caste, agricultural labour (rural) and casual labour (urban) households experienced decline in poverty on par with the total population, scheduled tribe households fared badly in both segments" (Sundaram and Tendulkar, 2003: 5263). In other words, during the post-reform period the economic situation of tribal population in India got worsened. This is confirmed by the present study about tribals in Kerala.

Because of the crisis in agriculture, the worst sufferers were the SC/ST population who mostly depend on agriculture. "This would definitely hit the reservation groups particularly scheduled castes and scheduled tribes and backward classes as these are the sections which largely rely on agriculture" (Chalam, 1994: 37). This is what happened particularly for Adivasis in Kerala.

No wonder the life of Adivasis became miserable due to the problems in agriculture, which was a direct consequence of globalisation. "For tribals, globalisation is associated with rising prices, loss of job security, lack of health care and tribal development programmes" (Raj, 2005: 9). This is true of Adivasis in other parts of India too. They were adversely affected by globalisation. "In the economic sphere globalisation had a negative impact on the Adivasis, causing migration of youth to big cities, effecting not only a brain drain but also a generation drain" (Tirkey, 2004: 6). The reference is to Adivasis in Jharkhand and Madhya Pradesh, who migrated to the cities in the north when they lost work in the agriculture fields in their own places. In Kerala also a similar phenomenon has happened to Adivasis in Wayanad district, who have migrated, not to the cities for jobs but to places like Gudalur in Tamil Nadu for agricultural operations. This was destroying even their sociocultural life.

Wayanad, with the highest concentration of tribals and with major cash crops of coffee, pepper and tea, is a typical example of how agricultural crisis has affected the livelihood of tribals. "The huge fall in prices has savaged the district of Wayanad. Pepper price has fallen from Rs 27,000 a quintal in 1997 to about Rs 5,400 in 2004. Grown in 70,000 hectors, farmers and their labourers suffer" (Sainath, 2004). In real terms the collapse in price of pepper and coffee affected the labourers who depended on them and Adivasis were the worst sufferers. One of the main reasons for this situation was the dumping of imported goods, which was directly due to liberalisation. "In 2002–03 India imported 6,204 ton pepper without any import duty. It was a big increase from 1241 tons in 2001–02. Besides, 15,100 ton pepper was imported from different countries"; remember pepper is a major cash crop in Wayanad (Deputy Minister in Lok Sabha, 2003).

"The agrarian crisis and farmers' distress in Kerala over the past one decade are loosely linked to the neo-liberal policy regime implemented in the country in the recent past. The association between the two is more in the regions of the state which are heavily dependent on export oriented crops, such as coffee and pepper. The worst affected are the small farmers, as they are more vulnerable to crop and price fall. They find it extremely difficult to pay back the loans they have incurred, in order to grow crops and survive" (Mohankumar, 2006: 1553).

The present study has shown that the annual working days of tribals drastically decreased since there was no employment in farm estates of crash crops where most of them worked. The farm estates were not operating since there was no remunerative price for these products. Price fell due to liberal imports of the same crash crops as part of liberalisation policy of the government. Thus this policy has directly reduced the employment opportunities of the tribals. Thus globalisation has adversely affected the livelihood of the tribals in Kerala.

Availability of Essential Commodities for the Tribals

Food security by means of availability of essential commodities is very important for the people, especially the poor. So, essential commodities like food grains and kerosene are provided to the people through the Public Distribution System (PDS) at subsidised rates. This has been a great source of food security for the marginalised people like Dalits and tribals. As part of livelihood issue for the tribals, the study has examined the availability of essential commodities for them during the last ten years.

It was found from the study that 83 per cent of the tribal households had ration cards and most of them regularly purchased essential commodities from PDS. This was confirmed from the villages selected for case studies. In other words, the tribals fully depended on PDS for their food requirements especially since their traditional sources of food from forests and their own farmland became scarce. But during the past few years the situation has changed.

The study has shown that 57 per cent of the tribals get cereals (rice/wheat) from private shops and only 49 per cent get it from PDS. The rest get from their own farms. The reasons given are high price and poor quality of food grain. So tribals buy from private shops at high price but of good quality and sufficient quantity. This means that the tribals either spend more on food or they do not buy it enough. Either way their nutritional needs and living standard are adversely affected. Thus they do not get the benefit from PDS as they used to get earlier, and by depending on the private shops for essential commodities, their food security is badly affected. The study has also revealed that the tribals spend more on essential commodities like kerosene and rice than on fish, meat, milk and grains, since about half of them (49%) purchase them from private shops.

Globalisation and Availability of Essential Commodities

The experience of the tribals with regard to essential commodities through PDS is confirmed by the national level situation of PDS as followed by the government in the post-reform period. The study analysed from secondary sources the macro-situation of PDS and how it has affected the people, especially the marginalised groups all over the country, and how it is related to the globalisation policy of the Central Government. Although there was increase in food production and food stock, there was decrease in distribution through ration shops.

Table 6.5

Agricultural Production and Distribution in Kerala (in crores of tonnes)

Year	*IAP per cent*	*Food Production*	*Food Stock*	*Ration Distribution*
1991–92	–2.0	16.84	1.96	2.08
1992–93	4.1	17.95	1.79	1.88
1993–94	3.6	18.43	2.81	1.64
1994–95	4.5	19.15	2.60	1.40
1995–96	–2.1	18.04	2.26	1.53
1996–97	9.5	19.94	1.98	1.83
1997–98	6.2	19.23	2.36	1.78
1998–99	8.2	20.30	2.63	1.84
1999–2000	–1.5	20.89	3.08	1.70
2000–01	–4.6	19.61	3.55	1.21

Source: CMIE, May 2001, Economic Survey 2000–01 (Kunjikannan, 2001: 64).

The table shows that the distribution through ration shop has been steadily decreasing during the period 1991–2001, though there was steady increase in food procurement and even production. Food-stock steadily increased from 1.96 crore tonnes in 1991–92 to 3.55 crore tonnes in 2000–01, while the distribution through ration shop has steadily and steeply decreased from 2.08 crore tonnes in 1991–92 to 1.21 crore tonnes in 2000–01. This means there was a decline in the purchase of food grains from the ration shop by the people. "After the reform, off-take of wheat and rice as a percentage of the allocation has shown considerable decline. In the years from 1990–91 to 1992–93 this percentage was generally over 80 per cent but in the next three years from 1993–94 to 1995–96 it came down to below 50 per cent in the case of wheat and to a little over 60 per cent in the case of rice". "... since, the difference between the Public Distribution System (PDS) retail prices and market prices became marginal, the not so poor left the PDS, and owing to unaffordable prices the poor cut their consumption. The resultant effect on nutrition and hunger had to be borne by the people in direct proportion to their poverty. One study revealed that the families of landless labourers and marginal and small farmers reduced their off-take by over 50 per cent" (Teltumbde, 2005: 5). "... During two years of reforms there was 8.43 per cent fall in per capita availability of cereals and 12.02 per cent fall in that of pulses" (Teltumbde, 2000: 5).

One main reason was that as part of the globalisation policy the Central Government reorganised the ration distribution among people on the basis of Below Poverty Line (BPL) and Above Poverty Line (APL) and steadily increased the price of ration goods. As a result, people did not have purchasing power to buy even the ration food grains. It is a clear case of how the poorest people in India are hit by the policy of reducing the subsidy as part of liberalisation.

The table 6.6 shows the steady increase of price of ration rice and wheat. In 2001 the government increased the price by 30 per cent after creating the BPL-APL categories. This price increase has seriously affected the food security of SC/ST people.

Table 6.6

Wholesale Price Increase of Ration Food Grain in India (Rs/quintal)

Year	*Rice*			*Wheat*
	Normal	*Fine Super*	*Fine*	
1.4.91	289	349	370	234
28.12.91	377	437	458	280
11.1.93	437	497	518	330
1.2.94	537	617	648	402
1.6.97 APL		650	750	450
BPL	350	350		250
1.12.97 APL		700		250
BPL	350	350		250
29.1.99 APL		905		650
BPL	350	350		250
1.4.99 APL				682
1.4.2000 APL		1180		900
BPL	590	590		450
1.7.2001 APL	830			610
BPL	565			610
	300			610

Source: FCI documents (ibid.).

Retail price of food grains given through Public Distribution System (PDS) also got increased during the reform period.

Table 6.7

Retail Price Increase of Ration Food Grain in India—1991–2001 (Rs/kg)

Items	1990	1991	1992	1993	1994	1997	1999	2000	2001*	2001**
Rice	3.28	3.78	3.94	5.02	6.84	7.20	9.65	12.50	12.50	9.00
Wheat	2.26	2.56	3.02	3.80	4.35	5.00	7.20	9.75	9.75	6.00
Sugar	5.25	5.56	6.90	8.40	9.15	—		12.60	13.25	
								BPL	ONLY	

Source: Ration shops (Kunjikannan, 2001: 69).

According to the table the retail price of rice and wheat increased four-fold and of sugar three-fold during the said period. Between

1991–2001 the price of ration food grain increased ten times. This had impact on the intake of ration food grain since the card holders did not have the purchasing power to buy ration food at the increased price. The government increased the price of ration food continuously so that it was able to reduce its subsidy on food as part of the requirements of globalisation process guided by WTO.

In the case of Kerala, the price of ration grain was raised nine times in the 1990s. The price of Rs 3.20 per kilogram of rice in 1990 was increased to 13.20 in 2000. This is clearly the globalisation period. As a result, sale of food grain decreased considerably. The people who are not able to purchase food grain are the marginalised people like Dalits and tribals. The tribals particularly were affected by this as was shown from the case studies. It was said that the tribals did not get the full benefit of ration shops due to high price, less quantity and poor quality. In other words, the globalisation policy directly affected the in-take of essential commodities of the tribals, and their poverty increased.

Table 6.8

Sale of Ration in Kerala (in metric tonnes)

Year	*Rice*	*Wheat*
1995	11.32	4.23
1996	14.04	4.92
1997	16.17	3.52
1998	16.39	4.58
1999	13.58	2.71
2000	6.14	0.62

Source: FCI documents (Kunjikannan, 2001: 101).

The decrease in the purchase of ration goods is shown in the table. The sale of rice through Public Distribution System (PDS) got reduced from 16.39 metric tonnes in 1998 to 6.14 metric tonnes in 2000. Similarly sale of wheat through PDS has came down from 4.58 metric tonnes in 1998 to 0.62 metric tonnes in 2000. The reason is that the purchase of these commodities by consumers was low.

"Wherever economic reforms were implemented, they have worsened the situation of the masses of poor people in absolute as well as relative terms" (Teltumbde, 2000: 17). The Dalits and the tribals were hit the hardest in India. "While those at the centre have benefited from globalisation, the already marginalised have often been left further behind" (Fernando, 2006: 19).

The government was consistently increasing the price of ration goods so that it could reduce its subsidy on PDS. For this, they also classified people as BPL and APL and reduced a substantial quantity of essential goods for APL category. Reducing the subsidy for and withdrawal from PDS by the government is necessitated by the conditions of WTO and IMF. As government's withdrawal from the socioeconomic sphere is part of the proclaimed policy of globalisation, it is enforced on PDS meant for the poorest of the poor in our country. Thus they lose the food security they have been enjoying so far without substituting alternative source of income or food. The tribals in Kerala are mostly illiterate and unskilled, and their traditional coolie work has been substantially reduced as an aftermath of the liberalisation policy of the government. When their purchasing power is lowered even to buy the existing commodities in PDS, they will be all the more hard-pressed to buy at a higher price. Naturally they are compelled to buy essential commodities from private shops at a higher price. This badly affects their spending on other essential needs of the family like health and education. Thus globalisation has adversely affected the tribals, the most vulnerable section of the people of Kerala.

It was shown how livelihood of the tribals in Kerala were adversely affected by the policy of globalisation. Earlier land, employment, and essential commodities through PDS were means of livelihood and life support systems for tribals. Land is no more a source of livelihood as they are deprived of it. Their wage from employment in farmland and estates of cash crops got reduced substantially as agriculture was not remunerative with low price for agricultural products. With limited income, the PDS was a great source of support for the tribals especially when their employment and other source of livelihood got reduced. But as the government was steadily increasing the price of food grains distributed through PDS, they were forced to depend on private shops for the same, probably at a higher price and with reduced quantity. With their low employment and subsequent low purchasing power, the in-take of the tribals naturally was less than in earlier times. This had an impact on their life and health. Thus the policy of globalisation has adversely affected the food security of the tribals, and in turn their life itself.

Poverty and misery of tribals have increased as an outcome of globalisation. When there is lack of sufficient work as mentioned above, their main source of income is lost. Since they have hardly any other source of income, they face deprivation and starvation. Besides, their suffering further increased due to the rise in price of essential commodities including those provided through the Public Distribution System. Since the tribals do not have purchasing power they are not able to procure food even from the ration shop. Naturally they suffer from poverty and malnutrition. In the words of one who was interviewed, "as a result of globalisation the Adivasis face unemployment, poverty, disease, starvation and death. They are on the verge of extinction." Another remarked, "Adivasis are the first victims of globalisation." Thus from the data from survey case study, interview and secondary sources it can be concluded that globalisation has caused more poverty and misery for tribals in Kerala than in the pre-reform period.

Analysis of the Impact of Globalisation on the Sociocultural Life of the Tribals in Kerala

This section analyses the result of the study on the impact of globalisation on the cultural and religious practices of the tribals in Kerala together with data from secondary sources. There are five areas covered in this section—cultural and religious practices, health, education, tribal women and organisation of the tribals.

Cultural and Religious Practices of the Tribals

To understand the effect of globalisation on culture and religion, questions were asked in survey method about the effect of television and cinema on the culture, values and religion of the tribals. More than half of the respondents (51%) stated that television and cinema had negative impact on the family structure and customs of the tribals. The areas influenced by them are their lifestyle, fashion, dressing, language and food pattern. Forty-three per cent of the respondents also said that the traditional tribal values like sharing, common ownership, and cooperation had declined due to the modern media. The study also showed that more than half of the respondents (55%) are of the opinion that they had lost the religious and non-religious tribal customs and practices due to the influence of media. This was also confirmed by the tribals from the villages chosen for case studies.

In the village of Mully in Palakkad district, people used to watch video films throughout the night for days together so that 'Koothu", their main cultural form had totally gone out of use. The same village reported that tribal values like cooperation and sharing had got diminished due to the influence of modern media and life. In Paliyakudy in Idukky district the tribals admitted that modern media and life had destroyed their customs so much that the new generation did not even own them up. They added that only a traditional dance connected with death has survived. The village of Mully and Paliyakudy specially reported that advertisements in television and films had developed consumerism among the tribals by motivating them to buy non-essential commodities with their meagre income, thus curtailing the consumption of essential food items. In Paliyakudy many tribals had got into the debt trap by buying such non-essential consumer goods. Since advertisements in electronic media are very much part and expression of globalisation it can be said that globalisation has adversely affected the simple lifestyle, customs and religious practices of the tribals.

The respondents of personal interviews also confirmed that tribal culture has been adversely affected by globalisation and its vehicle of media and communication. "Given the sociocultural background, the tribals are influenced by consumerist culture," said a social activist. As a result of their contact with the mainstream culture they have started losing interest in their traditional lifestyle and religious practices. Tribal values of cooperation, sharing and family bond have been the first casualties. The process has been accelerated with modern media like television and cinema. The respondents also feel that modern media as part of globalisation has had a bad impact on the art and artefacts of the tribals. Thus the personal interviews largely confirm the result of the survey schedules, namely, that globalisation has had an adverse impact on the tribal culture. This is also endorsed by authors on tribal culture: "Globalisation is oppressive and would suppress local languages and cultures with its market forces" (Seabrook, 2001).

Some of those personally interviewed said that it was not possible to protect tribal culture from globalisation due to the following reasons: (1) Tribal identity and culture are already lost or are in danger of being lost to the mainstream culture. (2) Religious practices, dress style and even body features are changing. (3) The power of media can destroy the culture of the tribals. (4) People in power impose their culture on tribals. (5) Forest and forest produce, which were closely related to tribal culture, are disappearing. (6) Destruction of agricultural sector also has an indirect impact on their culture.

Most others who were personally interviewed were of the opinion that tribal culture could be protected from the impact of globalisation. They have given various suggestions to protect tribal culture and identity.

1. Tribal language, lifestyle and customs, arts and artefacts, and festivals should be encouraged and protected. The tribals should be helped and encouraged to value their tribal identity and culture.
2. The living environment of tribals should be restored. Land, soil, trees, forest, water, air and other natural resources should be made available to them. Land and food security should be provided based on sustainable development through farming based on natural manure, and bio-diversity agreement and benefit sharing should be implemented.
3. Developmental activities, which endanger their traditional way of life, should be given up.
4. Programmes envisaged in Panchayat Raj for tribals including self-rule should be implemented.
5. Tribal language should be used in lower primary school and tribal culture should be included in the school syllabus.
6. Cultural and artistic organisations should be formed to protect tribal culture. They should organise cultural 'melas', and NGOs and government could support them in such activities.
7. Encroachment and occupation of tribal land and areas by outsiders who destroy tribal culture should be prohibited
8. Tribals should be motivated to give up emulating the bad habits of upper class and caste and mainstream culture, particularly the use of drugs and drinks.

Taking into account the two views of the respondents about tribal culture given above, one would say that integration of tribal life into modern life should be fostered while maintaining the identity of tribal life and culture so that the tribals live and develop as tribals. If the good customs and practices of tribals are not kept up the tribals will lose their identity as tribals, which can create problems for the indigenous people as has happened in other parts of India and the world. Here the remark of an author is relevant. "If the unequal exchange that marginalises these tribals is to be reversed, then they must not be left in isolation, not even in the mistaken notion of preserving their tribal identity. This only marginalises them still further. For ethnic identity is dynamic, not static … . We believe that like every human identity, tribal ethnic identity too must be dynamic, and it actualises the human potential that is present in every human group. The danger, however, in romanticising them is to condemn them to primitivism …" (Heredia, 2002: 5177). In other words, preserving the tribal identity and culture does not mean that they are kept as museum pieces. Like all dynamic societies, tribal society also should interact with mainstream culture so that the dynamic aspect of the tribal culture is kept up.

What the study has revealed about the evil effects of globalisation on tribal culture and practices is confirmed by the experience of tribals in other places. According to Jeremy Seabrook, "Globalisation is oppressive and would suppress local languages and cultures with its market forces" (Seabrook, *Deccan Herald*, 2001). "Folk songs which are hundreds of years old and related to particular seasons and cycles of nature are disappearing under the impact of the commercial culture promoted by electronic media and cinema" (Bidwai, 2006: 52). The same author, while speaking of the evil effects of globalisation, also enumerates countless crafts, languages, music, notions of aesthetics and beauty of traditional communities that are getting lost under the impact of globalisation all over the world. Thus the effect of globalisation on the cultural life of the tribals in Kerala is a reflection of what has happened and is happening all over the world.

Health Situation of the Tribals

The study has brought out the health situation of tribals in Kerala in the post-reform period vis-à-vis the pre-reform period. This section analyses the data with the support of secondary data.

Health is an important parameter for social development. From the survey study we understand that 93 per cent of the household members of the respondents are in good health reflecting the good health index of Kerala. A negligible number of tribals suffer from rheumatic fever and other ailments. Sixty-eight per cent of the respondents' families witnessed death due to old age, while 32 per cent did not have death at all in their families during the last ten years. The case study of three villages also confirmed this good health index of the tribals in Kerala. But one aspect which the government and NGOs should give attention to is that a significant 44 per cent of the respondents did not know about immunisation of their children. Greater awareness needs to be created among the tribals about this.

In spite of the good health index, a pertinent question related to globalisation is how the tribals maintain this good health index and where they get medical treatment from. While 56 per cent of the tribals still go to the government hospital, a sizeable 16 per cent go to private hospitals. If we add the 12 per cent going both to government and private hospitals, more than 25 per cent go to private hospitals in total. In contrast ten years back hardly 3 per cent of the respondents went to private hospitals for treatment. While more than 65 per cent went to the government hospitals ten years back, the figure has reduced to 59 per cent today. The reasons they have given for going to private hospitals are non-availability of medicines, and lack of medical facilities and medical care. The case study of three villages also confirms the fact that tribals are increasingly depending on private hospitals. This increasing dependence of the tribals on private hospitals has implications for the effect of globalisation on the health of the tribals.

Lack of medicines and of proper medical treatment are the main reasons cited by tribals for not going to government hospitals. This is a phenomenon experienced by people in most government hospitals in Kerala. This means that the government may not be spending as much money for medicines and other facilities as it used to ten years back. Though the government has not decreased its expenditure on health it has not substantially increased the allocation either. With rise in prices of medicines and medical facilities the government will not be able to provide the same facilities and medicine without substantially increasing the allocation for health. The main reason is that as in the case of education, the government seems to be withdrawing slowly from health sector as part of the policy of globalisation. Thus, when the policy of globalisation is implemented it is the most marginalised sections like tribals and Dalits who are the worst sufferers.

Government Policies and Expenditure on Health Sector in the 1990s

The study shows that there is less medicine and medical care in government hospitals for tribals at present than there was ten years ago. The pattern of government expenditure on health may explain the reasons for this phenomenon. For this the annual expenditure of the central and state governments for the health sector during the period 1990–91–96, the period when globalisation process started, is examined.

Table 6.9

Expenditure for Health Sector in the Annual Plans of Central Government in the 1990s

Year	Total Developmental Cost (in crores)			Health Expense (in crores)		
	Central and States	Central	States	Central and States	Central	States
1990–91	40062	23511	16551	659 (1.65)	189 (0.8)	471 (2.84)
1991–92	39075	22839	16236	629 (1.61)	183 (0.8)	447 (2.75)
1992–93	39946	23958	15988	665 (1.67)	210 (0.88)	455 (2.85)
1993–94	44573	27942	16631	658 (1.48)	203 (0.73)	454 (2.73)
1994–95	48482	31186	17296	780 (1.61)	273 (0.88)	507 (2.93)
1995–96	54662	33518	21144	924 (1.69)	285 (0.85)	639 (3.02)

Note: Figures given in brackets indicates percentage.

Source: National Coordination Committee, "Arogyavum Agolavalkaranovum" (Malayalam), *Health and Globalisation*, Kerala Sastra Sahitya Parishad, Kozhikode, 2001: 51.

Though the percentage and the amount of expenditure for health has remained steady and has even increased slightly, it is not a substantial increase when we consider the rise in prices of commodities. With a marginal increase in expenditure for health, it would be difficult to maintain the existing health facilities in government hospitals.

Table 6.10

Share of Health and Education in Total Budget Expenditure in India

Five-Year Plan	Years	% of Total Plan Expenditure		
		Education	Health	Total
1. First Five-Year Plan	1951–56	7.86	3.32	11.18
2. Second Five-Year Plan	1956–61	5.83	3.01	8.84
3. Third Five-Year Plan	1961–66	6.87	2.63	9.40
4. Plan Holiday	1966–69	4.60	2.11	6.71
5. Fourth Five-Year Plan	1969–74	4.90	2.12	7.02
6. Fifth Five-Year Plan	1974–79	3.27	1.92	5.19
7. Sixth Five-Year Plan	1980–85	2.70	1.86	4.56
8. Seventh Five-Year Plan	1985–90	3.70	1.88	5.58
9. Eighth Five-Year Plan	1992–97	4.50	1.70	6.20

Source: PIRG, 1992: 16, Government of India, 1998, Raghava, 2002: 57.

The budget for education and health in Five-Year Plans upto the Eighth Five-Year Plan in 1997 reflects the decrease in their allocation. In fact, the percentage of plan expenditure for health decreased especially in the 1990s, the period of globalisation.

With increase in prices of medicine and medical equipments, decrease in expenditure on health will mean less medicine and medical facilities in government hospitals and primary health centres. The table shows a similar trend in education too. This indicates that the government is reducing its expenditure on these sectors. The health expenditure of the Central and state governments together was more than 1 per cent of GDP in mid–1980s, but since then it has been declining and is now only 0.9 per cent. In fact, the expenditure of Central Government alone at present is only 0.1 per cent of GDP (Ghosh, 2007). In the post-reform period this might be connected with the policy of globalisation under which the government is withdrawing more and more from social sectors. This was especially the case of states with poor economic growth. Kerala was one such state which was struggling to keep up even the earlier standard of good spending on health. Naturally poor people, especially the tribals, did not find even the minimum medicines available in government hospitals. The experience of the people has been that instead of getting medicines from the government hospitals and health centres, they were getting prescriptions to get medicines from medical shops. This shows that the government's policy of globalisation has adversely affected the health status of tribals in Kerala.

Privatisation of Health Sector

The study shows that even the tribals are increasingly depending on private hospitals. Many reasons like lack of medicine and proper treatment facilities were pointed out for this phenomenon. Their dependence on private hospitals is confirmed by the manifold increase of private health institutions especially in the 1990s. The following table shows the increasing trend of private hospitals in India:

Table 6.11
Private Involvement in Health Sector in India

	1951	*1971*	*1981*	*1996*
Hospitals	2,694	3,862	6,805	15,097
% Private	8	14	43	68
Beds (000s)	117	349	505	870
% Private	—	20	29	56
Doctors (000s)	61	153	266	504
% Private	70	68	71	76

Source: Dr. K.P. Aravindan, 'Kerala Arokya Mathruka Puthiya Noottandeleku', (Malayalam), Kerala Sastra Sahitya Parishad, Kochi, 2001: 123.

Though there was steady increase in hospitals, beds and practising doctors from 1951–1981 in India, the increase and its rate in the private sector was significant from 1981–1996. The same trend can be seen in Kerala also. While beds in government hospitals increased from 36,000 in 1986 to 38,000 in 1996 with 5.5 per cent growth, the increase of beds in private sector was from 49,000 in 1986 to 67,500 in 1996 with a growth rate of 40 per cent. During the same year there was 64 per cent increase in the number of doctors and 81 per cent increase in para-medical personnel.

With quantitative increase in health sector, modern scientific facilities like CT scan and Magnetic Resonance Imaging (MRI) scans, and the most modern surgical methods are provided much more in private hospitals than in government hospitals. No wonder an increasing number of people in Kerala approach the private hospitals for treatment. Sixty-two per cent of people in rural Kerala depended on private hospitals for medical treatment in 1996 (Kerala Health Model, 2001: 126).

The study has already shown that even the tribals are increasingly approaching private hospitals not only for the above reasons but also because of lack of even basic medicines and treatment facilities in government hospitals. The consequence is that they spend a substantial portion of their income on private hospitals, which should have been spent on food and basic needs. This means privatisation as part of globalisation has adversely affected the health needs of the tribals. In short, globalisation has made the life of the tribals more miserable than earlier. If the expense for health care of households in Kerala is analysed it can be found that expense for treatment has gone up considerably, especially in the 1990s.

Table 6.12

Expense of a Patient for One-Time Treatment in Kerala (in Rs)

Items	*1987*	*1996*	*Increase %*
Medicine	8.24	83.48	913
Fees	2.90	27.87	930
Others	5.41	51.87	859
Total	16.56	165.22	898

Source: Ibid., p. 151.

The above table shows that expense of one patient for one-time treatment increased from Rs 16.56 in 1982 to Rs 165.22 in 1996, which is 898 per cent. The increase in expense is due to a big increase in price of medicine, fees for the doctors and medical check-up.

Table 6.13

Per Capita Annual Expense of People of Kerala for Medical Treatment (in Rs)

Items	*1987*	*1996*	*Increase %*
Medicine	44.20	282.36	539
Fees	15.60	99.06	535
Others	29.12	167.44	475
Total	88.92	548.86	517

Source: Ibid., p. 151.

If the annual per capita expenditure for medical treatment for people of Kerala is examined, it is found that per capita expenditure increased from Rs 88.92 in 1987 to Rs 548.86 in 1996, an increase of 517 per cent.

Table 6.14

One-Time Expense for Medical Treatment of a Patient in Kerala in Different Health Centres (in Rs)

Treatment Place	*Expense*
House	46.55
Government Hospital	183.96
Private Hospital	195.71
Others	171.10

Source: Ibid., p. 152.

An interesting finding is that there is not much difference between expenses in a private hospital and in a government hospital, as is shown in the table 6.14. While the one-time treatment expense in 1996 for a patient in a private hospital in Kerala was Rs 195.71, it was Rs 183.96 in a government hospital. The main reason is that the patients have to buy most of the medicines from outside with their own money.

If this is the situation of an average patient in Kerala, the situation of the tribals is worse. They spend a substantial amount of money for treatment even when they go to the government hospital, since they have to spend money on purchase of medicine. It means even the government hospitals are not affordable for the tribals. Naturally they will go to private hospitals for better treatment.

The withdrawal of the government from health sector and subsequent dependence of the poor on private hospitals is also confirmed at the national level. The slow but steady withdrawal of the state from comprehensive primary health care supported by secondary and tertiary levels, has had an impact on the confidence of the people to access medical facilities that are being provided to them by the state. Many studies reveal that "increasing number of individuals from poor and lower income households are accessing private care facilities, irrespective of the cost they have to pay for the same, thanks to the dilapidating quality of public health care" (Raghav, 2002: 42).

Privatisation of even social sectors is a characteristic of globalisation. Since the Government of India is following the policy of globalisation with privatisation, it is slowly withdrawing from social sectors and is allowing private sector to take over those responsibilities. The people too will be forced to approach private institutions for basic services. In this case, the tribals will have to depend more on private hospitals than on government hospitals. Thus globalisation has seriously affected the health needs of the tribals in Kerala.

As the tribals started increasingly going to private hospitals, they were forced to spend more money in the 1990s than in earlier times when they depended on the government hospitals with much less expense. Thus the globalisation period has adversely affected the tribals in their health needs. "Kerala which was a model for achievement in public health is facing a crisis. We had this achievement with moderate expenditure. We were model for providing health for weaker sections. But now we are facing a crisis" (Aravindan, 2001).

In spite of good health index of the tribals the study has shown that they are increasingly depending on private hospitals due to lack of medicines and medical facilities, compared to the pre-reform period. This has not only affected the health of the tribals but also their living standard as they have to spend more on health and less on other essential needs. One main reason for poor health facilities in government hospitals is failure of the government to increase the spending on its hospitals since it is gradually withdrawing from health sector as part of its policies of privatisation and globalisation. The secondary data substantiate and support this conclusion. The expenses of individuals on medical treatment have increased manifold, while the spending on the health sector by the government has not increased proportionately. People worst hit by this situation are the tribals. So it can be reasonably said that globalisation has adversely affected the health system of the tribals in Kerala.

Education of Tribal Children

Since quality education is a must to cope with globalisation, the study examines the effect of globalisation on the education of tribal children. While the state prides itself on a literacy rate of above 90 per cent, its tribal population has only 57 per cent literacy. If the 43 per cent of illiterate tribals have to be made literate at least for the future generation, quality elementary education should be given to tribal children. All the more needed is education and training to equip them to face globalisation creatively. But the situation of tribal education is pathetic. The study shows that the average drop-out rate of tribal children from 1st to 10th Standard was 39 per cent. The main reasons the respondents gave for the dropping out were low standard of government schools, financial difficulties and high fee structure in private schools. Most of the tribal children were studying in government school since the tribals cannot afford private schools. These are of poor quality without even basic facilities. The school system in general is not adapted and made attractive to tribal culture and life. And if they are not even of reasonably good standard, tribal children will not have any incentive to attend these schools. These reasons explain the high drop-out rate among tribal children. The government and NGOs can remedy this problem by providing good schools and remedial education.

In the three tribal villages chosen for case study, the drop-out rate in lower primary schools is considerably low since they function in the village itself and since lumpsum grant and noon-meals are provided regularly. But in higher classes it is goes up to 50 per cent. One reason cited was the long distance from home to school since high schools are usually located far off from the villages. In one village, children have to travel 30 kilometres to reach a high school, that too without regular and proper transport facilities. Thus schools have to be set up nearer to tribal villages to attract and retain children in schools. Secondly, the government should see to it that tribal children get lumpsum grant at the beginning of the academic year as the tribal families will not be able to buy the study materials for the children otherwise. Besides, noon-meals also should be provided from the beginning of the academic year since it will be a great incentive for the tribal children.

Privatisation of professional colleges is a special feature of the post-reform period in Kerala. When the government permitted engineering and medical colleges to be started by private agencies, many such institutions came up in Kerala. They charged very high fees, which made these professional institutions inaccessible to the majority of the ordinary citizens, especially the marginalised groups like Dalits and tribals. This has become a very controversial issue which has polarised the leftist government on the one side and the private professional institutions on the other. What is obvious in this privatisation process, which is part of the policy of globalisation of the Central government and which is followed by the state government, is that tribals will not be able to access professional education which equips people with information technology and bio-technology. Thus globalisation, which has led to privatisation, has deprived the tribals of any chance of professional education. They will be all the more marginalised when they are not able to get even elementary education in government schools, which are getting neglected due to increasing privatisation of school education.

Those who were personally interviewed expressed their opinion about the possible benefits of professional courses and information technology, which are an integral part of globalisation. Some of them said that the tribals were not able to get these benefits since they were not equipped for them and since their basic education itself was of low standard. Today those who are educated and qualified forge ahead, while those who are not, fall back in the labour market. Since tribals are not educated they are pushed back further. Besides, according to the respondents, tribals will not be able to compete with others since competition is alien to tribal culture. "Tribals do not have the capacity to face the competitive aspect of globalisation", said one social activist. So culturally, socially and educationally they are handicapped.

As part of the policy of globalisation there is a tendency in the government to withdraw from the social and the educational fields. This is seen in the reduction of the expense on education or not increasing it (Table 6.10). This can affect the standard of education, especially in government schools. Since most of the tribal children go to government schools, their education is affected and they become victims of globalisation. Secondly, as part of globalisation, privatisation is taking place in every field including education. It is a common sight in Kerala that private English medium schools are functioning very close to the government schools, with the result that the government schools do not have enough children and slowly get closed. It is obvious that tribal children are not able to go to private schools due to high fees. Thus privatisation as part of globalisation is adversely affecting the education of tribal children.

In a globalised India and Kerala, educationally and even technically qualified people are needed for any employment and economic advancement. In the present situation, the tribal children are not able to get even basic school education, leave alone technical or higher education. Naturally, they will be pushed back and will become even more economically poor than at present. Thus the poor people like tribals and Dalits are becoming poorer as a result of globalisation. To remedy this situation and to help the tribals, especially their future generations, to face the challenges of globalisation they have to be given quality education including technical education. That is how education can be made a source of socioeconomic progress even for the tribals.

Situation of Tribal Women

The high status of women in any society is an indicator of the healthy social situation of the society. In tribal societies in general, women had a high status. But with the modernisation of these societies in relation to the mainstream society, the situation has changed. Women are losing the socioeconomic and cultural position that they enjoyed earlier. This study examined the impact of globalisation on tribal women.

By many socioeconomic characteristics, tribal women are much behind tribal men. In our study while 32 per cent of men were illiterate, 41 per cent of women were illiterate. The education at school level for boys was higher than that of girls. There were more widows (10%) than widowers (2%) in the tribal society in our study. Occupational distribution of tribals showed that 32 per cent of men were unemployed while the corresponding figure for women was 45 per cent. As a result, 57 per cent of tribal women did not have non-agricultural income, in comparison to 44 per cent of men who did not have such income. These data show that in comparison to men, many tribal women do not have family and financial support systems.

With regard to livelihood, our study found that employment for tribals in general has decreased considerably during the last ten years, more so for tribal women. While women had on an average 107 working days per year ten years back, they have only 48 days at present. The reasons for this drastic decrease was the same for women as for men. They were totally dependent on agricultural farms and estates for work. When the price of agricultural products crashed due to the liberalisation policy of the government, agricultural operations and subsequently employment declined. The tribals in general, especially women, were adversely affected. When women had work, they had some income to manage their own needs and those of the family. This gave them certain independence, freedom and self-respect. But when they did not have income from wage they had to totally depend on men whose income also got reduced due to the same reason. This means that globalisation has adversely affected the life and livelihood of tribal women more than of men.

Although there was no decrease in wages of women during the last ten years but there was no equal pay for the same type of work. Our study reveals that average wage per day for men was Rs 68 while for women it was only Rs 40. This put the women at a more disadvantageous position than men. Besides, though there was no decrease in wages, there was no increase in wages either during the last ten years. Since the price of essential commodities was regularly rising, the tribal women and men would not be getting the same amount of commodities with the same income. As a result, the quality of life of women was more affected than for men, as women often took greater responsibility over the household needs than men. Besides, the substantial reduction of working days during the last ten years has added misery to the tribal women.

The study of three villages also confirms the above data of considerable decrease in employment of women during the last ten years.

Women are not as economically independent as they used to be since they do not get enough work or equal pay. Forest produce used to be a source of income particularly for women in olden times. Now they hardly get any such income. Even for firewood and fodder they have to travel long distances since the forests are destroyed, and in hilly areas they have a hard time collecting water. As a result, all the three villages reported that the workload of women had increased during the last ten years of globalisation with the resultant effect on their health too.

The data given above showed how tribals are increasingly depending on private shops for essential commodities, since the quantity and quality of these commodities given through PDS had considerably reduced and their prices were steadily increasing. This was particularly affecting women, since women have greater responsibility than men to provide food for the family members. Since their meagre income from reduced working days is spent on buying essential commodities from private shops they are forced to forgo many other household things, and this in turn adversely affects their quality of life.

Because of the increasing hardships caused by the economic reasons described above, the social life of tribal women is also badly affected. The status they enjoyed in tribal society does not exist anymore. They are also exploited in many ways. One of the villages of the case study reported sexual exploitation and a few cases of unwed motherhood. The health of women is also getting affected more than that of men as they are increasingly depending on private hospitals. When women spend their meagre income on medical treatment in private hospitals, their basic needs of essential commodities for the family are getting compromised and thus it is often the women who suffer most in the family.

The analysis of the study shows how tribal women are adversely affected by the policy of globalisation. Their livelihood is seriously hampered since they do not have sufficient employment opportunities as a result of the liberalisation policy of the government. They suffer more than men in the family since essential commodities at moderate prices are not available through PDS as they used to be. So they are forced to go to the private shops to get these essential goods at higher prices. This is due to the reduction in subsidy for PDS as the government is gradually withdrawing from the field of food security for the poor. Under same policy of privatisation and globalisation the government is withdrawing from the field of health also. Here again women are worse sufferers than men for their medical and health needs. In short, the liberalisation, privatisation and the policy of government's withdrawal from health and educational fields, have adversely affected the tribal women.

Organisation of Tribals to Face the Challenges of Globalisation

The earlier chapters tried to find out what could be done to help the tribals to face the evils of globalisation. The role of the government, NGOs and the non-tribal people was mainly discussed. Now the question as to what could be done by the tribals themselves to face the challenges of globalisation becomes relevant. To answer this question, it is important to know the nature and extent of collective action that the tribals have in their life. In other words, the study tried to find out the present level of sociopolitical participation of tribals, and to suggest the future collective action the tribals could take up based on that. This section will include data about participation of tribals in sociopolitical organisations and possible kinds of collective action that the tribals could take up to face the challenges of globalisation.

With regard to social participation, the study has revealed that the vast majority of tribals (61%) are not involved in any social participation. This shows the low level of sociopolitical consciousness among tribals in Kerala where the general population has one of the highest political consciousness and participation in India. Therefore, it is not easy for tribals to organise themselves for any political action. They have to be made aware of it and to be initiated into it gradually.

Among those who have some sociopolitical participation a large proportion (39%) are involved in political parties, not as active workers of political parties but as affiliates to political parties or their ideologies. Other areas of social participation on a priority basis are "kudumbashree", self-help groups (SHGs) organised by the Panchayat, cooperative societies and SHGs organised by NGOs. Since a sizeable number of tribals participate in SHGs organised either by the Panchayat or NGOs, they could be made available for largest regions and for a greater number of people, and tribals could be encouraged to join them.

With regard to grass-roots level political participation the study has shown that a substantial portion of tribals (80%) attended Gram Sabha meetings and majority (54%) attended "Oorukoottam", the tribal Panchayats. The case studies in three villages in three districts also confirmed the result of the survey study that vast majority of the tribals attended the Grama Sabha and "Oorukoottam". This shows that Panchayati Raj was beneficial for tribals especially under the People's Plan Campaign. The reasons could be that tribals benefited from schemes like housing and drinking water, and the Panchayat was localised to the tribal situation. For more active and meaningful participation in Panchayat bodies, training programmes in Panchayati Raj can be conducted for tribals. Also tribal developmental programmes can be channelled through the Panchayat.

The study has found that only 44 per cent of the respondents participated in any tribals organisations other than Panchayat and SHGs. This means that the organisational strength or experience is low among the tribals of Kerala. It further means that it is difficult to build up tribal organisations or movements among them. But the heartening fact is that vast majority (73%) are willing to join such tribal organisations. Therefore, efforts could be made to organise the tribals. As part of the organisational participation, the respondents were asked whether they had participated in any tribal agitations. It was reported that only 34 per cent of tribals participated in agitations at either local or state level. This further confirms the low level of political consciousness and participation of tribals to demand their rights. Again it is an indication that it is difficult for the tribals to get organised on the tribal issues. But the hopeful sign is that a great proportion of the respondents (77%) were ready to participate in agitations.

About the question whether they wanted to work in a political party or an a non-party political organisation to fight for the tribal cause, 63 per cent wanted to work in a non-party political organisation. The tribals in all the three villages chosen for case study also expressed their willingness to join non-party political organisations. This shows that tribals are more inclined to work in a non-party tribal organisation to achieve their development and welfare. Since there is no state-level non-party tribal organisation other than Adivasi Gothra Maha Sabha (AGMS) known and established in Kerala, it is easy for AGMS to get acceptability and accessibility among the tribals in Kerala. All the more so since most tribals were willing to work collectively and organisationally for their rights and justice in a tribal organisation and not in a political party. In other words, a non-party political organisation can help the tribals in their needs especially to counter the evil effects of globalisation.

The respondents of the personal interviews also had a similar opinion regarding the type of organisation tribals should have in order to face globalisation. Many said that tribals should be organised to form a powerful sociopolitical movement to resist globalisation and defend themselves against its onslaught. For this, awareness should be created about the adverse effects of globalisation, and the tribals should be motivated to work collectively. They should be organised as far as possible on a non-party political basis. Their organisational strength should be used to pressurise the government to correct the policies of globalisation harmful to them and make policies that are helpful to them. The government should be pressurised to give the benefits of globalisation to the weaker sections like tribals and Dalits.

There were opinions among the respondents that tribals themselves should work in their own way to counter globalisation. They should try for diversification of jobs instead of depending on the traditional occupations. For this, they should develop their human resources through alternative forms of life and labour. They should also avoid consumeristic tendencies of the West, which are a by-product of globalisation. Those who have land should cultivate local products for food self-sufficiency and sustainable development, with green manure for food crops. Almost unanimously all the respondents agreed that tribals should organise themselves and collectively work to face the effect of globalisation by protecting their rights over their livelihood and culture. There is need of a powerful movement of tribals to face the challenges of globalisation. However there was disagreement regarding the type of organisation.

In the survey and interview among the tribals and non-tribals the respondents were overwhelmingly of the opinion that a non-party political organisation (NPPO) would help tribals to face globalisation in an effective way. The Adivasi Gotra Maha Sabha (AGMS) led by Ms. C.K. Janu, a NPPO, was the most known Adivasi organisation which brought up the tribal issues and problems in the forefront of Kerala's political scenario. Therefore, the respondents were asked to assess the role and function of AGMS.

Most respondents said that AGMS as a NPPO organisation of tribals was good and it should be welcomed. C.K. Janu took the tribal issue to the national and even international scene, and she thus represented the emerging power of people. It has relevance and great scope to work effectively for tribals. "Janu really raised the issues of Adivasis in Kerala before the public in the state and even India", said a social activist in the interview. "Janu emerged as the voice of the suffering and exploited Adivasis in Kerala", said another. AGMS can give hope to the Adivasis in the state for coming together on a common tribal identity. However the respondents were divided in their opinions about AGMS.

While appreciating the great contribution AGMS has made, the respondents also mentioned its limitations and its failures in certain areas. Many felt that it should have a stronger district/state-level organisational structure and network. Some felt that it has not succeeded in bringing up a second level leadership of tribals while many others said that its activities do not reach the grass-roots level and therefore its popular base and support have to be widened. As regards Ms. C.K. Janu, many respondents opined that she had not a got wide influence in all the districts. These felt that the AGMS should have a broad outlook and it should work for the unity of all tribals and tribal organisations. Many suggested that they would like to cooperate with good organisations in civil society for the development of tribals.

Most of those who were interviewed were of the view that AGMS had not got a popular mass base. The organisation was concentrated mainly in Wayanad district, that too among one or two tribal communities only. "Even in Wayanad AGMS has not got much root", said one activist from Wayanad. "AGMS keeps a distance from other sections of people", said another in the interview. What a group of tribal students from Attappady in Palakkad district said in the interview is striking: "The tribals at Attapady do not know who Janu is and what she does. She will be effective only if she goes to the people in other districts and mobilises them for AGMS". This was confirmed by tribals included in our survey and case study. Thus many thought that AGMS did not have enough organisational base to lead and sustain a powerful movement of tribals, especially to face the dangers of globalisation. However it could succeed if it mobilised at least the major tribal communities in various districts and strengthened its grass-roots level base and organisational structure in a democratic manner. But given the fact that there were over thirty-five tribal communities it was not easy to bring all of them together in one organisation. The identity of each community was too strong to come under the banner of one organisation. In fact, there were about a dozen organisations of tribal communities in Kerala. So, as a practical solution, many suggested a federation at the state level, of various organisations of tribal communities, on the lines of the Adivasi

Ayika Samithi, which is a federation of several organisations in Wayanad district.

However, given the limitations of the most marginalised group in the state, AGMS will find it extremely difficult to do this work of building up a strong state level organisation. Support and assistance of existing organisations of tribal communities, social activists, academicians and people's organisations of other marginalised groups are vital for such an organisation. AGMS should be open to this vision if it has to make a breakthrough in building up a powerful organisation.

This section analysed the data from survey, case study and personal interviews about participation of tribals in sociopolitical organisations and found that the vast majority of tribals in Kerala do not have any experience in participating in sociopolitical organisations including tribal organisations. Those who had some experience were involved in SHGs and Grama Sabhas of Panchayat. But most of them expressed willingness to work together and even participate in agitations organised by tribal organisations to face the challenges of globalisation. They also preferred a non-party political tribal organisation, and not political parties, and so they were open to work with Adivasi Gothra Maha Sabha (AGMS), which hand led the state-level agitation for land, provided it built up a wider and deeper popular base and was open to collaborate with all other tribal organisations with the support of various organisations of civil society.

This chapter analysed the data collected by the study about the impact of globalisation on tribals in Kerala with the support of secondary data. The analysis covered the data on the effect of globalisation on the livelihood of tribals including employment and availability of essential commodities, and sociocultural life of the tribals including religio-cultural practices, health, education, condition of tribal women, and organisation of the tribals. The secondary data confirmed the major findings of the study and showed how the results of the survey study were related to the policies of globalisation adopted by the government across the country at both micro and macro levels.

7

Strategies and Suggestions to Counter the Effects of Globalisation on the Tribals

The present study has shown indisputably that globalisation has adversely affected the life and livelihood of the tribals in Kerala. Most of them had lost their land long ago and even those who have land do not find it a source of livelihood since cash crops which many of them have cultivated do not fetch sufficient income for them. Besides, since land is already used for cash crops, it is not available for food crops for their sustenance.

Since there is no profitable price for cash crops like coffee and tea as a result of the liberalisation policy of the government, the tribals who depended on agricultural farms or estates for their employment found their working days drastically reduced and their means of livelihood adversely affected. Compared to the pre-reform period their wage for agricultural labour also did not increase during the post-reform period.

Added to this, prices of essential commodities from public distribution system increased so much as a result of the policy of globalisation that the tribals increasingly bought them from private shops with adverse impact on their food availability and security. As a result, poverty and misery leading even to starvation deaths increased among the tribals. As was shown in the study their sociocultural life have also got adversely affected, by the modern media like television and videos, which have become powerful vehicles of globalisation.

Health and education are badly affected as the government is showing tendencies to withdraw from these sectors by reducing its spending on them. Since privatisation is the policy of the government, health system in India and Kerala is getting more and more privatised with the result that even the tribals, the most marginalised group in Kerala, are forced to depend on private hospitals for their medical treatment. With their already meagre income, tribals are being further squeezed by the mounting medical expenses. With low employment, low income and shrinking availability of forest products for fodder, food and water, the tribal women are the worst sufferers due to lack of proper food and free medical treatment. In such a situation they are also being exploited by non-tribals. Thus the tribals were found to be badly affected by the policy of globalisation initiated by the Indian government. Now the natural question is how the tribals can face globalisation and save their life, livelihood and culture. In other words, what could be the alternative strategies for tribals to counter the effects of globalisation in this situation? The study sought the opinion of tribals themselves about this question. Data was collected through personal interviews of tribals in the villages chosen for case studies and from their responses in the interview schedules. The responses from all these sources were compiled and were presented in the previous chapter. Based on the analysis and data the study in this section explores the alternative strategies and suggestions for the tribals to counter the effects of globalisation. This will be done under the broad headings which were followed all through this study namely, alternative strategies for livelihood, sociocultural life including health, education, status of women, and organisation of tribals.

Means of livelihood is vital and basic for any people, especially the marginalised, who often need to struggle to live and survive. The study has examined land, employment and availability of essential commodities as the source of livelihood for the tribals in Kerala. The suggestions will cover all these areas.

Distribution of Land to the Tribals

Since land is a necessary means of livelihood for tribals and since they were unjustly deprived of it over the years, land should be an important factor for their development. This is all the more so in a globalised world when they do not have any of the other source of livelihood which other sections of the population have.

Almost all the respondents of our study were of the opinion that land should be distributed to the tribals to help them to face globalisation at least in a limited way. The reasons stated by those personally interviewed are the following: Firstly, much of the land of the tribals in Kerala was alienated because of non-tribals and the faulty policy of the government. The people and the government of the state have an obligation to give back what was taken away. Secondly, till the tribals get equipped for alternative avenues of job, land can be a viable means to cultivate their food crops. This is all the more so, since the tribals do not have employment opportunities as a result of globalisation. Therefore, land can be a means of minimum subsistence to tide over the bad effects of globalisation. Thirdly, land is the basis of tribal culture, and so it is needed to preserve and sustain their culture and customs, which are threatened by globalisation. Therefore, the study recommends strongly to the government to distribute land to the tribals at the earliest as it had promised long ago. Land should be given in close-by places to form a village, not in scattered places. The land should also be sufficient and viable to meet part of their food requirement.

Merely distributing land is not enough to fulfil the obligations of the government towards the tribals. They need to be supported to cultivate it and to use it creatively, since they do not have enough capital to invest in land. Some of the tribal communities may not be familiar with developed methods of cultivation and their traditional methods may be too primitive to be economical today. This means the government should make suitable arrangement for them to get easy financial and technical help for a proper method of cultivation. This need not be a big problem for the government since there are many schemes and projects of the Central and state governments which are meant for the tribals and which are often not made use of. If the government can make a package using various tribal schemes, sub-plans and tribal component plans and coordinate them creatively, it can be of real assistance to the tribals. The Department of Tribal Welfare and the "Oorukootams" of the tribals can implement such schemes for the development of agriculture.

Our study also discussed the nature and type of cultivation. Since our study showed that 53 per cent of tribal households resorted to commercial farming, many respondents of personal interview suggested that the tribals should be encouraged to cultivate food crops. Subsistence farming has been reduced to 13 per cent at present from 28 per cent ten years back. This has is implications in a global economy. Tribals who depended on their land for their food crops started to cultivate cash crops and to purchase all food products from the market. Even the villages chosen for case study had increasing tendency to cultivate cash crops. Since the price of cash crops fluctuates and often falls below the remunerative level as it has happened now, cultivating cash crops cannot be a reliable source of income especially in a globalised market. Secondly, the tribals can get essential food items from their land if they cultivate food crops and the land can then become a source of food security. Though the choice of crops should be left to the tribals, they could be motivated to go for food crops rather than cash crops.

There were differing opinions in the study about the method of cultivation suited to the tribals. Some advocated purely traditional methods of cultivation, while others were for modern methods of cultivation. The study showed that only a small section of tribal households use modern methods of cultivation; the rest use traditional methods of cultivation. However, since most tribal communities are still using very primitive methods of cultivation, a combination of traditional and modern methods of cultivation is recommended. Progressive and self-sustaining methods of cultivation traditionally used by the tribals should be preserved and organic farming with green manure could be encouraged. Better varieties of seeds and suitable crops could be slowly introduced. Mechanisation of agriculture should be preferably avoided since land has to provide jobs for the family members and should also be financially viable. Constant guidance from the Tribal Welfare Department and "Krishi Bhavan" (agricultural centre) will be very useful for the tribals.

In short, distribution of land will be only the first step for the sustainability of tribal life. Durable programmes for helping and guiding them for viable cultivation are equally important otherwise, given the background of the tribals in Kerala, the purpose for which land is distributed will not be served. Though this is primarily the duty of the government, it can also get the support of NGOs and tribal organisations. The latter can cooperate with and complement the efforts of the government for ensuring greater effectiveness and people's participation. In fact, the study revealed that NGOs have assisted the tribals to modernise their agriculture much more than the government agricultural department. Therefore, NGOs have a creative role to play in helping tribals adapt modern methods of cultivation to their life and culture. However it is the government which should have a greater role in developing an integrated plan to improve tribal land and its mode of cultivation.

Implementation of Tribal Forest Rights Act, 2006

It is recommended that the government should make necessary rules and legal structures to implement the provisions of "The Scheduled Tribes and other Traditional Forest Dwellers' Recognition of Forest Rights Act, 2006", so that the tribals in Kerala get the benefits of the Act, including ownership of forest land and the right to collect minor forest products. As part of forest rights, tribals could be employed as forest guards. Tribal communities could be allowed to participate in protecting forests and its resources as is being done successfully in the state of Orissa (Fernandes, 1987).

Creating Employment Opportunities

The study has found that a glaring effect of globalisation on the tribals in Kerala is the drastic decrease in their employment opportunities during the last ten years of the globalisation period. The survey, case studies and personal interviews revealed and reinforced this fact. Since the tribals lost their employment they lost their source of livelihood, especially since they do not have other sources of income. Thus poverty and starvation increased among the tribals. It was also shown from the analysis that decrease in the number of working days of the tribals was due to the policy of liberalisation of the government. If so, the government has a duty to provide alternative job opportunities for the tribals, the most vulnerable section of society. This is because the right to livelihood is closely related to the right to employment. Providing employment will be one way of helping the tribals to face the adverse impact of globalisation.

In a globalised economy the government seems to be shirking its responsibility of creating jobs for people. The industries increasingly controlled by the private sector will not be able to provide jobs for the tribals since they are not skilled to work in industries. This means that the tribals can find employment mainly in the primary sector, viz., agriculture. One example of employment creation is the Attapady Hills Areas Development Society in Palakkad district, which is a huge scheme initiated by the government to generate employment for the tribals. To generate employment for the tribals, agriculture which was shown to be facing a crisis, should be revived. In Kerala, for the tribals, this refers to cash crops like coffee and tea. A basic requirement for the revival of agriculture is ensuring remunerative price for agricultural crops. As the price of agricultural crops crashed due to the imports of foreign agricultural products as part of liberalisation policy of the government, such policies should be changed to support agriculture, which can in turn provide employment to marginalised groups like tribals and Dalits.

It was shown that agriculture is facing faces a crisis throughout India. Large-scale suicide of farmers is one clear indication of this crisis. To revive agriculture, which has been the backbone of Indian economy, the Central Government needs to make drastic changes in its agricultural policy. Economic reforms that are more in favour of industries and are at the expense of agriculture will lead to pauperisation of large sections of people, especially Dalits and tribals. There should be a multi-pronged strategy to revive agriculture. Firstly, liberalisation policy of the government allowing duty-free or dutyless agricultural products should be changed to support agriculture in our country. For this sufficient control in import and export duties and customs should be introduced so that national agriculture is protected. The government should not hesitate to support its farmers in spite of the globalisation policy. Western countries are massively subsidising their agriculture and if they can do that in spite of the regulations of WTO and IMF, India too can support its farmers for whom it is a vital means of livelihood. No globalisation policy can be pursued leaving the large sections of farmers to their fate. Secondly, to make the farmers competitive in a globalised world, they should be given the necessary support and subsidies from the government side. Thirdly, increased investment in agriculture, at least at the rate of the pre-reform period, for providing irrigation, soil conservation measures, and remunerative price for crops, should be ensured. The government which gives many facilities to industry through export promotion measures and through creating investment climate, cannot neglect agriculture, the life-line of millions of people in the rural areas of India.

Ensuring Essential Commodities at Low Price through Ration Shops

Since land is not a source of livelihood for the majority of the tribals, and since their employment opportunities have been considerably reduced because of globalisation, they have no means of livelihood. As a result, the tribals in Kerala are facing poverty and in some cases even starvation. At this juncture, the government has to step in to provide food security to the tribals by making essential commodities available through PDS at affordable prices. Since the tribals are rated below poverty line, they deserve to get essential commodities distributed through ration shops.

Our study revealed that the vast majority of tribal households in Kerala depended on Public Distribution System (PDS) for their essential commodities before the reform period. This means that PDS was a real support for their life especially when traditional sources of food from forests and land became scarce. The situation changed after economic reform was introduced in India. According to the study majority of the households at present buy cereals from private shops instead of ration shops. This is revealing especially since the economic situation of tribals deteriorated due to decrease in their working days. In fact, more tribals should have depended on PDS but just the opposite has happened. The reasons given for moving away from PDS are high price of food grains distributed through fair price shops and their poor quality. The analysis has shown that after the reform period started the government has been consistently raising the price of essential commodities due to the policy of globalisation, so much so that the tribals did not have the purchasing power to buy food grain even from ration shops. This means that tribals spend either more on food or do not buy enough of it. Thus they do not get the benefit of PDS and their food security is affected. This explains the high poverty and even starvation deaths among the tribals. Such a grim situation demands that the government provides essential commodities to the tribals at affordable price, especially since they belong to the BPL category. Since it is the policy of globalisation pursued by the government has brought about this deteriorating food situation, it is duty-bound to help the tribals to face the adverse impact of globalisation by ensuring sufficient food materials at reasonable price.

Protecting the Tribal Culture from the Impact of Globalisation

Our study has shown that cultural life of the tribals in Kerala has been adversely affected by globalisation. When they were alienated and in many cases uprooted from land, the basis of their culture was destroyed. Through their contact with people of mainstream culture they not only lost many tribal practices and values like community living and sharing, but they also tended to imbibe the bad habits of mainstream culture like consumerism and drinking. The modern media, particularly television and cinema, replaced tribal cultural forms, religious practices and lifestyle so much so that the modern generation of tribals had no interest in and even knowledge of their traditional practices, customs and traditions.

Three main suggestions which came up from the respondents of the study to preserve tribal culture are, first, to keep away tribals from mainstream culture, second, to help them to fully integrate with mainstream culture, and, third, to help them to adapt themselves to mainstream culture. The proposal to keep the tribals away from the mainstream culture is not possible as they are already living and working with and among people of mainstream culture. Majority of them find their livelihood in employment provided by the agricultural farms and estates of non-tribals. Once they are kept away from them they will not have any means of livelihood, especially since the majority does not have land for cultivation. That means they cannot have any life and existence without the help of the non-tribals. Besides, in the globalised world where countries and culture are interdependent, tribals in one state cannot be kept separate from the rest of the people. Their economic, political and social life being closely inter-mingled with that of the non-tribals, they cannot have a separate territorial and cultural identity.

The second view is that they should be integrated fully into the mainstream culture so that they are also able, as was said by a respondent, "to enjoy the good things of modern life". This was only the opinion of a small minority and does not take into account the values of tribal culture and the need of preserving it. The third view is that they can be helped to adapt themselves to modern life even by preserving the culture and practices of tribals. In other words, they will be adapting themselves to mainstream culture rooted in their own culture and identity. For this, ways and means should be devised for preserving the traditional practices and customs of tribal culture and equipping the tribals to face modern life in a globalised world. The study subscribes to this third view, i.e., helping tribals to preserve their culture and at the same time equipping them to face modern life in a globalised world. It recommends the following concrete suggestions based on the survey and case study methods and on the suggestions from the respondents during personal interviews.

1. Tribal customs and life styles, art, artefacts and festivals should be protected. For this the tribals should be taught to value their tribal identity and culture through studies, seminars and training programmes. In addition to these, cultural and artistic organisations should be formed to protect tribal culture which should organise cultural 'melas' consisting of traditional tribal cultural forms, art, music. NGOs can play a vital role in this effort and the government should support and supplement the efforts of the NGOs and tribal organisations in this regard
2. Tribal culture and cultural forms should be included in the school syllabus so that the educational system itself nurtures and supports tribal culture.
3. The living environment of the tribals should be restored. For this, land, soil, trees, forest, water and other natural resources should be made available to them and they should be allowed to live close to nature and the natural habitat. The cultivation of land by the tribals could be based on sustainable development by using organic farming and natural manure.
4. Developmental activities which endanger the traditional way of life and culture of tribals should be avoided.
5. "Oorukootam", the traditional tribal Panchayat should be established wherever it is possible, so also tribal self-rule. These sociopolitical structures will supervise the activities and life of tribals according to tribal culture and customs and will also be able to resist the onslaught of globalisation on tribal culture.

6. Encroachment and occupation of tribal land by non-tribals who destroy tribal culture should be prevented by legal measures enforced strictly. Under no circumstances should outsiders be allowed to control the life and culture of the tribals. This is important to check the adverse influence of globalisation on the culture of the tribals.
7. Tribals should be encouraged and motivated to give up and resist bad and harmful habits and practices, values, and lifestyle typical of the globalised world, which have become part of the mainstream culture. Consumerism is one example. The study showed that even tribals get influenced by advertisements on television and they buy non-essential consumer goods with their meagre income, thus often falling into a debt trap. They should also be made aware of the evil effects of drinking and taking drugs which are very much prevalent in the mainstream culture. Modern media like video and television which are the concrete mirrors of globalisation should be discreetly used without replacing the religious and cultural practices essential to the tribals.

While the tribals should be encouraged to keep away from the evil effects of global culture and even the mainstream culture, they should be helped, as far as possible, to adapt themselves to a globalised world. As the world is changing very fast tribals cannot be expected to remain isolated. In fact, the study has shown that an overwhelming majority of tribals do not want to be isolated, but to be integrated with the mainstream society. Secondly, any society including tribal society needs to keep its dynamic character. However this dynamism should primarily come from within by using and developing its own sociocultural life. At the same time such sociocultural changes cannot take place without integrating changes and realities outside. Thus the tribals should be helped to preserve their tribal identity and culture, and also to integrate the good aspects of mainstream culture. The government and NGOs can do a lot in this matter.

Providing Health Facilities for the Tribals

The study indicated good health index of the tribals reflecting the good health of the population of Kerala. But there is sufficient indication to show that globalisation as shown in the privatisation policy of the government has affected the health situation of the tribals. This is seen by the increasing number of tribals going to private hospitals at present whereas ten years back very few of them went to private hospitals. The main reasons for the shift are non-availability of medicines and lack of medical facilities and medical care. This is because the government is not spending enough to maintain government hospitals; rather it seems to be withdrawing from health field as part of the policy of globalisation. It is instead allowing private sector to take care of the health need of the people. When the tribals with their frugal means go to the private hospitals, they spend the money which they would have otherwise spent on food and other essential commodities. Thus the tribals have been adversely affected by globalisation and the government has a duty to help them to tide over this adverse impact. The suggestions emerging from the study are the following:

1. As an effect of globalisation medical facilities in government hospitals are found to be less available to the tribals now than in the pre-reform period. So the government should allot sufficient funds especially for tribals so that medicines and facilities are available to them, who are the most marginalised group in our society. If this is not done, the tribals will depend even move on private hospitals as they do now and will be spending more on health than what they can afford, which will lead to poverty and starvation. Therefore, the government should actively help the tribals to overcome the adverse impact of globalisation on their health.
2. Where there are no public health centres the government should start one for the tribals, so that their dependence on private hospitals could be reduced.
3. The study has revealed that almost half of the tribals did not know about immunisation. This is disturbing in a state where the health index is very good. The government should take special care to spread awareness about immunisation among the tribals. NGOs can help the government in this effort.

Providing Basic and Technical Education for Tribal Children

All the respondents of the study of the survey and case study emphasised the need of both basic and technical education for the tribals to face the globalised world. But they differed on the type of education suited for the tribals. It is a fact that technical skills and quality education are necessary to cope with a globalised world. Those who have them thrive both in India and in the world. But the tribals have neither, and they cannot acquire technical skills unless they have quality basic education. The study has found that quality education is not available for most of the tribal children in Kerala. As a result, illiteracy rate among them is very high compared to that of the state. Worse still is the drop-out rate among tribal children from 1st to 10th standard. The reasons given by the respondents are low standard of government schools, financial difficulties and high fee structure in private schools. Since most tribal children depend on government schools, their standard should be of high quality. The government should give utmost attention to providing good infrastructural facilities, ensuring regular teachers and building up a conducive cultural atmosphere in schools where predominantly tribal children study.

Basic Education

The mainstream education is not at all adapted to the culture and life of the tribals. Besides, the quality of education available to the tribals is of very poor standard. No wonder there is high drop-out rate among the tribal children. It is in this background that the people have suggested 'Kanavu' type of education for tribal children. This is based on tribal culture and lifestyle, it has, to a certain extent, succeeded and proved to be a model education. But the study showed that there is also one section of the people who are critical of the 'Kanavu' model of education. Their main concern is whether such a type of education, though very effective, can be replicated for the tribals all over Kerala since there is a practical difficulty in spreading such a type of education. Secondly, when modern education in the era of globalisation is becoming more and more sophisticated and complicated, the question is raised as to how far students with 'Kanavu' education can cope with globalisation. The answer, based on the study, is that a combination of both these types of education could be adopted for tribal children. For this, the good elements of 'Kanavu' type of education can be integrated with the modern education. Besides, some important elements of tribal culture, customs and life style can be brought into the mainstream education.

Specific recommendations to improve the education of tribal children based on data from survey and case studies and personal interviews are the following:

1. Lumpsum grant and noon-meal should be given right at the beginning of the academic year. If they are delayed, as it often happens, the two most important incentives for the tribals will be missing, and naturally children will be dropping out of schools.
2. Adequate infra-structural facilities like good classrooms, furniture, audio-visual aids and playground should be provided generously to all the schools where tribal children are studying.
3. There should be high schools reasonably close to tribal hamlets so that accessibility becomes by itself an attraction, especially since tribal habitats are in hilly and forest areas.
4. Tribal language be used in primary schools since Malayalam is a foreign language for most tribal communities. This possibility should be explored and studied by anthropologists, NGOs and the government.
5. Tribal culture and customs should be included in the school curriculum and syllabus so that an atmosphere in which tribal children feel at home prevails in the schools which they attend. Tribal arts, cultural forms and games could also be included in the youth festivals in schools and colleges. These measures will help tribal children to study and survive in schools.
6. Wherever possible tribal teachers should be appointed in schools where tribal children are predominant.
7. Once quality education is ensured, modern techniques like computer and communication skills could be introduced simultaneously.
8. The above mentioned measures should be adopted for the tribal children in aided schools also.
9. In unaided private schools in tribal areas preference should be given to tribal children through a policy of reservation, fee concession, extra coaching and other facilities. Private schools cannot shirk their responsibility to the socially and economically disadvantaged sections of our population.

Many of these suggestions need not be a big problem for the government since there are already provisions for the education of tribals under tribal sub plan and special component plans of both Central and state governments. What is needed is determination of the government and its machinery to implement them in letter and in spirit with a consideration for a people who are the most deserving as they are the most exploited in Kerala society. The government is morally obliged to do this in order to help the tribals to counter the adverse effects of globalisation and to face it creatively and productively.

Technical Education

Once basic education is ensured, tribals will be prepared and equipped to take on technical education which will give them the skills to face a globalised world. There was general agreement among all the respondents that technical education should be given to the tribals as this will enable them to diversify their employment potential. But what is the type of technical education most suited to the tribals? Highly sophisticated technical education will not be suitable since the tribal children at present are not getting quality education to equip them for professional education. Therefore, technical education related to their traditional forest-based occupations should be fostered like basket-making and bee-keeping, which are the most suited to the tribals. Technical training in agriculture-related occupations and even agro-industries could be the other areas that can be explored for tribal children.

Based on the data from personal interviews the study also recommends regular training and capacity building for the tribals. It can include learning about tribal identity and culture which can help them to respect and value their own culture. Capacity building consists of providing various skills related to the traditional occupations of the tribals like basket-making and bee-keeping, agriculture-related occupations like vermin compost and mushroom farming, and industry-related training like welding and wiring.

When a specific question was asked about the use of information technology for the tribals to face globalisation, especially since it is closely linked to the process of globalisation there were divergent views among the respondents, both tribals and others. Some said that it was totally alien to them while others recommended it to avoid their being further marginalised. Even if the latter view is taken, the tribal children with their poor quality of education may be ill-equipped for information technology. Therefore, the first step should be to impart quality basic education. Together with it information technology through computer education could be gradually introduced for the tribal children.

Adopting Special Programmes for Tribal Women

Our study has shown that the socioeconomic situation of tribal women has deteriorated during the last ten years due to negative effects of globalisation. Therefore, the following proposals are made based on the study:

1. *Providing employment opportunities for tribal women:* The study has revealed that women have only a small number of working days per year at present compared to the pre-reform period. So their income has decreased and alongside their independence and sociocultural status has got reduced. That means globalisation has adversely affected the status and economic freedom of tribal women. Therefore they should be provided with employment which is basic to all their other needs. Any effort to increase the means of livelihood for tribal women would benefit all the tribals since women are responsible for the entire family.
2. *Distribution of land*: If the tribals are given land, as was promised by the government, women can cultivate essential food materials in them. Working in their own field is better suited to women than to men who can go to far off places for work. So land is both a source of employment and livelihood.
3. *Proper wages for women*: Payment of equal wage both for men and women for the same type of work will be another measure which will benefit women. The average wage of women at present is much lower than that of men in many areas of Kerala. This gender disparity should be rectified with equal wage, and the government should take the initiative to fix a just wage for women. There is also need of periodic revision of minimum wages for tribal men and women, especially since there was agricultural depression in Kerala due to globalisation.
4. *Giving greater access to forest products*: Our study showed that the workload of women has increased manifold since forest produce and fuel and fodder are not available. Tribal women should be permitted to access forests for firewood and fodder, where ever there are forest. Speedy implementation of provisions of Tribal Forest Rights Act 2006 will particularly benefit tribal women.
5. *Ensuring essential commodities at moderate prices through Public Distribution System (PDS)*: Providing essential commodities through ration shops is relevant for tribals in general, but it helps

women more than men since women have the responsibility of preparing food for all the family members. If they have to depend on private shops for these commodities, their share of food will be reduced. The government should ensure sufficient food materials made available through PDS.

6. *Providing sufficient medical facilities for women*: The study has shown how tribals are increasingly going to private hospitals instead of government hospitals, since there are not enough medicines and health care facilities in government hospitals. Women and children need more medical facilities than men, and so they should be adequately provided with these facilities. The government should provide medicines and good medical facilities in government hospitals and primary health centres rather than withdrawing from health field as part of the policy of globalisation.
7. *Giving education for tribal women*: The study has shown that tribal women are less educated than men. Also the educational level of tribal boys is higher than that of girls. This is different from the situation in Kerala where girls have equal level of education as boys. Adult literacy programme could be taken up for tribal women by the government and NGOs. Facilities for education of girls should be increased by setting up schools near their villages, infrastructural and academic facilities should be ensured in schools, and supplementary education for tribal students, particularly girls should be provided. In fact, if proper facilities and conducive atmosphere are provided girls will do equally well or even better than boys education, as is the experience in Kerala.
8. *Providing social protection for tribal women*: The study has also pointed out social problems of tribal women like unwed motherhood and widowhood. Though they are not widespread there is need to take measures to protect tribal women who are increasingly vulnerable to insecurity from outsiders in a globalised society. The basic solution lies in providing livelihood, education and health care which have already been discussed above. Once they are taken care of, the government should give legal protection to the tribal women from non-tribal intruders. NGOs and tribal organisations also can take measures to protect tribal women and to make them aware of outside exploitation.

Strengthening the Organisational Capacity of the Tribals

Almost all the respondents of the study agreed that tribals should organise themselves and work collectively for their rights over livelihood and culture. Most of the remedies suggested above can be effected only if the tribals are organised. So there is need of a powerful organisation or movement of tribals at the state level to work for the cause of the tribals.

Now the question arises as to what type of organisation would be effective for the tribals—an organisation affiliated to a political party or an organisation on a non-party basis. Most of the respondents of the study are of the opinion that the tribals should organise themselves on a non-party political basis. The situation of India and Kerala today seems to support this view of the tribals due to the following reasons: Firstly, if the tribals are organised under the banner of political parties they will not be able to keep their unity and identity. Since there are many political parties each will try to bring the tribals under its fold. Thus tribals will be divided on party line as is happening all over India. This naturally weakens the cause of tribals as tribals. Given the low economic and social status of tribals, non-tribals will be controlling the party and the tribals too. Tribals will not be able to get into leadership positions and they will be used as mere vote banks. Besides, the tribal cause will be only one among many issues for a political party. Secondly, the trend today in India and the world is that the marginalised people organise themselves on their cultural identity. Thus Dalits organise themselves as Dalits and tribals as tribals. In other words, liberation and development of tribals should be in and through tribals themselves.

Though the tribal respondents preferred to work in a non-party political organisation of the tribals, it does not mean that tribal organisations based on political parties should be ignored. Political parties have a definite role to play in a democracy, and in Kerala most major political parties have their own tribal organisations. In fact, the survey has revealed that the largest number of Adivasis (12%) belong to the Adivasi Kshema Samithi of CPI(M) and they are active among the tribals. Besides, non-party political organisations will have many practical problems like organisational network, structure, function and leadership, and therefore, on their own they may find it difficult to counter the effects of globalisation. So it is advisable that tribal organisations on a non-party basis collaborate with tribal organisations of political parties on issues connected with globalisation. Issue-based collaboration and networking among all organisations working with the Adivasis including those of political parties is the ideal. This need not be an impossible task since fishworkers in Kerala collaborate with unions of political parties and non-party organisations on issues relevant to the fisheries sector, especially those connected with globalisation. In other words, effort should be made to muster all organisational strength available among the tribals to defend themselves to face the adverse impact of globalisation.

If the tribals are to be organised under a non-party political organisation, the question as to which organisation would be able to lead them becomes pertinent. Most of the respondents acknowledged that Adivasi Gothra Maha Sabha (AGMS), which spearheaded the state-level agitation in 2001 in Trivandrum and the agitation at Muthanga in Wayanad District under the leadership of Ms. C.K. Janu, could be one such non-party political organisation to lead the tribals in Kerala to face the onslaught of globalisation. Based on the study it looks that AGMS could be a rallying point for the tribals to organise themselves. There are many reasons for this argument:

First of all, AGMS took up the basic issue of land before the government, organised agitations at the state level and made the government and the general public aware of the plight of the Adivasis. For the first time it forced the government to give an assurance to distribute land to the tribals. This was not a mean achievement considering the acute unorganised and economically backward situation of the tribals in Kerala. Thus it has opened up the possibility of the tribals in Kerala to organise at the state-level and demand their right. No other tribal organisation has so far emerged as an organisational force in Kerala, much less the tribal unions of the political parties. Secondly, AGMS brought name and identity for the tribals in Kerala. Earlier the public in Kerala were not even aware of the existence of tribals in the hill ranges of Kerala. Through AGMS and its agitations the people came to know how the non-tribals have exploited the tribals for years, and particularly how they were alienated from their land. Thirdly, it brought about a certain amount of networking of tribal organisations in a tribal style, though in a loose form, throughout the state. In short, AGMS for the first time gave hope and scope for a state-level tribal organisation in Kerala and thus crossed the first hurdle of forming a state-level organisation.

While acknowledging the importance of AGMS and appreciating its historical role in leading the tribals in Kerala the respondents are not unaware of its limitations. First of all, AGMS is concentrated in Wayanad district, that too among a few communities only. It is a great limitation that, being a state-level organisation, it has not got sufficient organisational base in other districts. It should have had its units and activities at least in the major districts where there is tribal population. Being an association of the most marginalised group which does not have any resource and personnel, it is not easy for AGMS to establish its presence in all the districts but being a state-level organisation it should represent tribals from major districts so that it is able to take up the issues of tribals in those districts.

Secondly, AGMS does not seem to have organisational network to lead and sustain a powerful movement of tribals against the dangers of globalisation. This is related to the first limitation. If there is a good mass base, there is a possibility of at least a loose organisational structure or network, which can further help to mobilise the tribals in wider areas and at a deeper level. For this, it could at least mobilise major tribal communities in various districts and strengthen its grass-roots level organisation in a democratic manner. Even this is not easy for an organisation of a marginalised group. It is here that the support and assistance from existing organisations, academicians, people's organisations of other marginalised groups and social activists become imperative. In other words, various organisations or forums of civil society should be made use of to build up a strong state-level organisation. AGMS should be open and willing to solicit cooperation from all like-minded people to make the organisation a powerful state-level movement.

Will this non-party political organisation be able to unite all the tribal communities in Kerala? According to the official figure, there are at least 35 tribal communities in Kerala and there are more than a dozen organisations based on community identities. Some of these communities are Hinduised so much that they consider themselves superior in status or purity than others based on caste. So there may be difficulty in bringing all these communities under one umbrella. In fact, Adivasi Gothra Mahasabha tried to do that but with limited success. Though such a unity of tribals could still be aimed at, a more viable option would be a federation of various community-based tribal organisations to be visualised at the state-level. For this to happen the leadership of

AGM and of other tribal organisations should be open and flexible to accept and assimilate various tribal organisations on an equal footing based on the criterion of tribal identity and unity.

If the tribals are organised as a non-party political organisation what should be the issues it should take up in the era of globalisation? To answer this question the respondents of our study were asked how to solve the problems arising from globalisation. The answers, though coming from a minority, reveal the fact that tribals are aware of the problems of globalisation. On a priority basis they are to reduce the price of food items, to increase the price of agricultural products, to change the import-export policy of the government, to change the present economic system meaning the globalisation policy of the government and to distribute land to the tribals. These are the issues to be taken up by the tribal organisation with the government, and public authorities, so that the government changes the policy of globalisation in favour of the tribals. This will be the way the tribals themselves could be working to face the adverse impact of globalisation.

The first suggestions for solving the problems of globalisation is to reduce the price of essential commodities distributed through PDS. The government has been steadily increasing the price of essential commodities during the post-reform period. It also restructured the PDS with the two categories of BPL and APL. The study has shown that these measures forced the tribals increasingly to depend on private traders thus endangering their food security and availability. So it is natural that the tribals want the government to reduce the price of essential commodities distributed through ration shops. The government had increased the price of these commodities since it wanted to reduce the subsidy for food materials, which is part of the policy of privatisation and globalisation. Since the food security of the tribals is affected due to the policy of globalisation, the government should take steps to protect a vulnerable section like the tribals from this adverse impact of globalisation. The tribals want the government to continue giving subsidies for essential commodities and not to withdraw from the areas directly connected with the basic necessities of the poor.

The next suggestion of the respondents is to increase the price of agricultural commodities. The tribals seem to have understood the relation between the decrease in price of agricultural commodities and liberalisation policy of the government. For the farmers to get a remunerative price, import should be curbed and support price should be given to agricultural products. As was indicated earlier, the liberalisation policy of the government has created a crisis in agriculture which employs about 65 per cent of the population in India. The government should rectify these lopsided policies and thus protect agriculture and its dependents. If there is remunerative price for farm products, farmers will restart agricultural operations, and Adivasis who depend on farming will get employment, and thus they will benefit. This is especially so in the case of cash crops like coffee and tea in Kerala, in which the tribals find work. If there is good price for the farm products, Adivasis who have land also will benefit from the sale of their own products. Therefore, the tribals want the government to change the export-import policy which is directly linked to globalisation so that the farmers and the marginalised groups like tribals and Dalits are able to face the negative effect of globalisation.

Another significant suggestion of the tribals is to have the present economic system, meaning the system of globalisation with privatisation and liberalisation, changed. This means the tribals are dissatisfied with the globalisation process which has made their life more miserable than earlier times. As the tribals from the villages selected for case study asserted, the policy of globalisation has destroyed their life, livelihood and culture. It should be drastically changed in favour of the marginalised and the majority of the people. A sizeable section of the respondents wanted land to be distributed to the tribals as a means of countering the effects of globalisation. When the tribals have lost employment and other means of livelihood, they feel that they could at least fall back on cultivation of food crops in their own land. This can also be a means of preserving their culture against the onslaught of globalisation.

Conclusion

This study on the 'Impact of Globalisation on Tribals' was conducted using quantitative and qualitative methods. It examined the impact of globalisation on the livelihood and sociocultural life of the tribals. Means of livelihood included land, employment and availability of essential commodities, while sociocultural life included sociopolitical life, cultural and religious practices, health, education and situation of tribal women. After analysing the effect of globalisation on these aspects, the study suggested some methods of countering the impact of globalisation on tribals in Kerala.

The study revealed that the livelihood of the tribals in Kerala has been seriously affected by globalisation. Their employment opportunities were considerably reduced during the last ten years of post-reform period since the tribals were depending on work provided by agricultural farms mainly of cash crops like coffee and tea. As a result of crash in prices of these commodities agricultural operations have almost been stopped. Tribals who depended on these farms were the worst sufferers. Reduction of price of agricultural crops was due to the liberal imports of these products from other countries, which was directly related to the liberalisation policy of the government. Thus one of the obvious effects of globalisation on the tribals in Kerala was their loss of work with the result of adverse impact on their livelihood.

Though economically very backward, the tribals had certain food security because of the public distribution system in Kerala. But the study has shown that a large section of the tribal households were buying cereals from private shops. The main reasons were the high price and poor quality of the PDS food grain. In the post-reform period the Central Government was consistently increasing the price of essential commodities with a view to reducing subsidy of the government as part of the policy of globalisation. The result has been disastrous for tribals, as they do not get food grains as they used to, especially when they are experiencing decreasing income. Thus globalisation has led the tribals to greater poverty and misery. The government has to change its policy of PDS in favour of the most vulnerable section of society.

The study also has found that the tribals are not getting health facilities as they used to get during the pre-reform period from the government hospitals. The reason is the policy of the government to withdraw from health sector as part of its policy of privatisation. So globalisation has badly affected the medical needs of the tribals. The policy of the government on privatisation of education at schools and at higher education level is adversely affecting the tribal children. Since they were already very backward in education they have not been able to come up and compete in modern education. The tribals are the worst affected section of the society due to the reduction in the government's spending on education. The government has a special responsibility to provide basic and technical education for tribal children so that at least the future generation is able to cope with the challenges of globalisation.

With regard to the sociocultural sphere, the study has shown that globalisation has adversely affected the religious and cultural life and practices of the tribals, so much so that they are getting uprooted from their cultural root and identity. The traditional status of tribal women has been badly affected when their employment opportunities were drastically reduced due to the globalisation policy. The non-availability of food grains in ration shops added to the woes of the tribal women and even children. In addition poverty and even starvation have led the tribal women to be victims of exploitation by non-tribals.

Since globalisation has adversely affected many aspects of the life of the tribals, the government and society at large has a responsibility to take protective measures for this marginalised group. The tribals also should pressurise the government to protect their rights against the currents of globalisation. For this, they should organise themselves as tribals and work jointly with all like-minded organisations to work for the tribal cause. Thus together with all organisations of civil society and even of political parties, tribals should work to counter the evil effects of globalisation. Awareness building, training programmes and non-formal education at the grass-roots level in districts where tribal presence is strong, are needed to empower the tribals. All tribal organisations should be willing to consolidate and work together for the goal of empowerment and development of tribals in Kerala. Activists, academicians and other persons from civil society should also be willing to give the necessary support to the tribals. However, ultimately it is through the tribals themselves that lasting development and liberation of tribals can be realised. Only then will the tribals in Kerala be able to face the adverse impact of globalisation and move together with all other sections of people, towards their socioeconomic development and emancipation.

Bibliography

Anthuvan, Victor Louis. 2006. *The Dynamics and the Impact of Globalisation*. Madurai: Amirtham Publications.

Aravindan, K.P. (Ed.). 2001. *Kerala Health Model in a New Millennium* [*Kerala Arogya Mathruka: Puthiya Noottandilekku* (Malayalam)]. Kochi: Kerala Sastra Sahithya Parishad.

Arun, L.K., Jayasankar, B. and Abraham, Kurian Mathew. 2001. Biodiversity Conservation and Livelihood Issues of Tribesfolk: A Case Study of Periyar Tiger Reserve. Thiruvananthapuram: Kerala Research Programme on Local Level Development, Centre for Development Studies, Discussion Paper No. 37.

Baburaj, K.K. 2001. Adivasi Struggle: A Feature and Translation. *Madhyamam Weekly*, December 7, pp. 29–30.

Baby, K.J. 1983. *A Play (Nadugadhika–translation)*. Bangalore: Visthar.

——, 1991. *Maveli Manram* (Malayalam). Thrissur: Current Books.

Beleena, M. 2001. Dr. Thera Continues his Struggle. *Mathrubhumi Weekly*, October 7–13.

Bhalla, Surjit S. 2003. Recounting the Poor: Poverty in India, 1983–99. *Economic and Political Weekly*, Vol. 38, No. 4, January 25, pp. 338–48.

Bhaskaran, 2002. *Life Story of C.K. Janu* [*C.K. Januvinte Jeevithakatha* (Malayalam)]. Kottayam: DC Books.

Bhaskaran, K. and Ammini. 2001. *What Globalisation Does to People's Health [Arogyavum Agolavalkaranavum* (Malayalam)*]*. Kochi: Kerala Sastra Sahitya Parishad.

Bidwai, Praful. 1996. Privatisation Perils: Bringing the State Back. *Times of India*, December 11.

——, 2006. *What Now to What Next, "What Next"?*. Vol. 1, No. 47, June.

Bijoy, C.R. 1999. Adivasi Betrayed: Adivasi Land Rights in Kerala. *Economic and Political Weekly*, Vol. XXXIV, No. 22, May 29-June 4, pp. 1329–35.

——, 2003. The Muthanga Struggle: An Analysis (Mimeo).

Boban, K. Jose. 1998. *Tribal Ethnomedicine: Continuity and Change*. New Delhi: A.P.H. Publishing Corporation.

Buckman, Greg. 2004. *Globalisation: Tame it or Scrap it? – Mapping the Alternatives of the Anti-Globalisation Movement.* London: Zed Books Ltd.

Carrera, Joan Carrera i. 2003. *Global World, Global Ethics*. Barcelona: Cristianisme I Justicia Booklets, December 2.

Chalam, K.S. 1994. Globalisation and Farmers. *The Modern Rationalist*, June-July.

Chaudhuri, Budhadev (Ed.). 1982. *Tribal Development in India*. New Delhi: Inter India Publications.

Cheria, Anita et al. 1997. *A Search for Justice: A Citizens Report on the Adivasi Experience in South India*. Bangalore: Jose Sebastian.

Chossudovsky, Michael. 1997. *The Globalisation of Poverty*. Malaysia: Third World Network.

Cithara, Paul. 2005. Kerala Farmers' Plight Getting Bad to Worse. *Indian Express*, October 8.

Committee, National Coordination. 2001. *Arokgyavum, Agola Valkaranavum* (Malayalam) (Health and Globalisation). Kozhikode: Kerala Sastra Sahitya Parishad.

CUTS. 2001. *Globalisation and India: Myths and Realities*. Jaipur: (Pro-globalisation booklet series).

Datt, Gaurav, Kozel, Valerie and Ravallion, Martin. 2003. A Model-Based Assessment of India's Progress in Reducing Poverty in the 1990s. *Economic and Political Weekly*, Vol. XXXVIii, No. 4, January 25, pp. 355–361.

David, James and John Desrochers CSC. 1998. *Dimensions of Globalisation*. Bangalore, Centre for Social Action.

Deccan Herald. 2000. December 11.

——, 2003. June 23.

Dev, Mahendra Rohini, Hensman (Ed.). 2005. Impact of Globalisation on Employment in India and the Response. Advocacy Internet, Vol. 7, No. 4, July-August, p. 2.

Economic Review. 1999. *Details of Schemes Implemented by KSDC for SC/ST*. Government of Kerala.

Fernandes, Walter and Menon, Geeta. 1981. *Tribal Women and Forest Economy*. New Delhi. Indian Social Institute.

——, 1987. *Tribal Women and Forest Economy: Deforestation, Exploitation and Status Change*. New Delhi: Indian Social Institute.

Franco, Fernando. 2002. *Ten Years of Liberalisation in India: Consolidation of a New Economic Elite*. VIKALP Alternatives. Vol. X. No.1. Mumbai: Vikas Adhyayan Kendra.

——, (Ed.). 2006. *Globalisation and Marginalisation: Our Global Apostolic Response*. Rome: Social Justice Secretariat, February.

Ghate, Ruchas. 1992. *Forest Policy and Tribal Development*. New Delhi: Concept Publishing Company.

Ghosh, Jayati. 2004. Liberalisation and Democracy. *Frontline*, Vol. 2, No.17, August 27.

——, 2007. Unhealthy State. *Frontline*, Vol. 24, No. 19, October 5, 2007.

Government of India. 2007. The Scheduled Tribe and other Traditional Forest Dwellers (Recognition of Forest Rights) Act, 2006. The Gazette of India.

Government of Kerala. 1998. *Bharana Report 1994–95* (Malayalam) (Administrative Report). Kerala Government Scheduled Tribes Development Department.

——, 2003. Scheduled Caste and Scheduled Tribe Colonies. Website: Kerala.gov.org, July 28.

——, 2003. Scheduled Tribe Development Department. Website: Kerala.gov.org, July 28.

——, 2003. Integrated Habitat Development Programme. Website: Kerala.gov.org, July 28.

——, 2003. Statement Showing the Allotment of Funds (Grant-in-aid) to Local Bodies Under Special Component Plan and Tribal Sub Plan. Website: Kerala.gov.org, July 28.

——, *Economic Review 2000*. Thiruvananthapuram: State Planning Board.

——, 2003. Report of Kerala Government sent to Central Government.

——, *Economic Review 2002*. Thiruvananthapuram: State Planning Board.

Heredia, Rudolf C. 2002. Interrogating Integration: The Counter-Cultural Tribal Other. *Economic and Political Weekly*, Vol. XXXVI, No. 52, December 28, pp. 5174–78.

Ilaiah, Kancha. 2003. Cultural Globalisation. *The Hindu*, February 22.

Information Bulletin. 2004. *Facts Against Myths*. Mumbai: Vikas Adhyayan Kendra, February-March.

——, 2004. *Facts Against Myths*. Mumbai: Vikas Adhyayan Kendra, April-May.

ISI Delhi occasional Dispatch. July 1997. Globalisation.

Iyer, V.R. Krishna. 2003. Atrocities on Adivasis-I. *The Hindu*, June 16.

——, 2003. Atrocities on Adivasis-II. *The Hindu*, June 17.

Jacob, Lukose. 1995. *Thudichetham* (Malayalam). Wayanad: Hilda Trust.

Jacob, T.G. 2005. Misery in an Emerald Bowl: Essays on the Ongoing Crisis in the Cash Crop Economy (Mimeo).

Jain, P.C. 2001. *Globalisation and Tribal Economy*. Jaipur: Rawat Publications.

Jha, Avinash. 2000. *Background to Globalisation*. Mumbai, Centre for Education and Development.

Johnny, O.K. 2001. *Notes of Wayanad [Wayanadu Rekhakal* (Malayalam)*]*. Calicut: Pappiyon.

Justice and Peace Commission. 2004. *Is India Really Shining? Vote with your Conscience Campaign*. Mumbai: St. Pius College.

Karunakaran, C.K. 2000. *Kanikkar* (Malayalam). Thiruvananthapuram: State Institute of Languages.

Kattakayam, Jacob John. 1983. *Social Structure and Change among the Tribals*. Delhi: B.R. Publishing Corporation.

Kothari, Rajni. 1998. *Globalisation: A World Drift*. Bangalore: CIEDS Collective.

Krishnakumar, R. 2000. Public Distribution System: A System in Peril. *Frontline*, September 20, pp. 97–100.

——, 2003. A Conflict in the Forest. *Frontline*, March 14, pp. 37–40.

——, 2003. The Muthanga Misadventure. *Frontline*, March 28, pp. 42–47.

Kunhaman, M. 1989. *Development of Tribal Economy*. New Delhi: Classical Publishing Company.

Kunhikannan, T.P. 2001. *Hunger, Poverty and Ration Rice [Visappu Daridryam Reshanari* (Malayalam)*]*. Kochi: Kerala Sastra Sahitya Parishad.

——, 2001. New Forms of Narmada Struggle. *Mathrubhumi Weekly*, May 20–26, pp. 10–12, 54.

Lazar, S. 1998. Globalisation and Culture (Mimeo). Bangalore: Indian Social Institute.

——, 1998. Impact of Globalisation on Culture (Mimeo). Bangalore: Indian Social Institute.

Lutheran World Federation. 2001. Engaging Economic Globalisation as a Communion (Mimeo). Delhi: Department for Theology Studies.

Madala, Bashir. 2002. *Unnatural Deaths* (Malayalam). Kalakaumuthi, January–February.

Mahanti, Neeti. 1994. *Tribal Issues: A Non-Conventional Approach*. New Delhi: Inter-India Publications.

Mathew, Thomas. 2002. *India Betrayed: Globalisation and Realignment*. Delhi: Centre for Social Studies.

Mathrubhumi, Daily. 2003. July 14.

——, 2003. October 11.

——, 2003. July 25.

——, 2003. May 3.

——, 2002. September 5.

——, 2004. July 4.

Mathur, P.R.G. 1996. Encyclopedia of Dravidian Tribes Volume 1. Trivandrum: International School of Dravidian Linguistics, pp. 87–89.

——, 1977. *Tribal Situation in Kerala*. Trivandrum: Kerala Historical Society.

Ministry of Welfare, Government of India. 1996. Workshop on Effective Implementation of Scheduled Castes and Scheduled Tribes (Prevention of Atrocities) Act, 1989. April 22–25. Hyderabad: Centre for Social Development National Institute of Rural Development.

Mohandas, M. 1992. Impact of New Settlers in the Western Ghat Region of the Socio-Economic Conditions of the Tribal Population: The Case of Wynad District in Kerala (Mimeo). Thrissur: Kerala Agricultural University.

Mohankumar and Sharma, R.K. 2006. Analysis of Farmers' Suicide in Kerala. *Economic and Political Weekly*, Vol. XLI, No.16, April 22, p. 1553.

Mundakayam, Gopi. 2002. *The Unknown Wayanad [Ariyappedatha Wayanad – Charithram* (Malayalam)*]*. Kalpetta: Sahya Publications.

Murickan, Ajit. 1997. *The New Economic Path: Trend and Impact*. Mumbai: Vikas Adhyayan.

——, 1997. *Globalisation and SAP: Trend and Impact: An Overview*. Mumbai: Vikas Athyayan Kendra.

National Commission for Scheduled Castes and Scheduled Tribes. Annual Report 1993–94.

NCAS. 2003. Alternatives to Globalisation. *Advocacy Internet*, Vol.5, No. 36, November-December.

Negi, S.S. 1986. *Tribal Welfare Development and Administration*. Dehradun: International Book Distributors.

Oommen, M.A. 1993. The Political Economy of Globalisation, "The Other Side".

Padmini, P.G. 2001. The Pulse and Rhythm of Forest Life. [*Kattujeevithathinte Spandanathalangal* (Malayalam)]. Thalassery: Akam Samithi.

Panoor, K. 1996. *Adivasis Who are Left Out* (Malayalam). *Mathrubhumi Weekly*, March 17–23, pp. 6–11.

——, 1963. *Kerala's Africa [Keralathil Africa* (Malayalam)*]*. Kottayam: National Book Stall.

——, 1990. *Children of the Western Ghats [Sahyante Makkal* (Malayalam)*]*. Kottayam: Sahitya Pravarthaka Co-operative Society Ltd.

Parsai, Gargi. 2006. *The Hindu*, September 26.

Pawar, Sharad. 2005. Statement in Rajya Sabha. *The Hindu*, November 27.

Payal, Kapadia. 2000. Tribal Girl Students Become Easy Prey in a Long-running Sexual Exploitation Racket. *Outlook,* July 10.

Peer, Chand. 2000. Globalisation: Its Bearing on Socio-Political Processes a Subaltern Perception. *Kerala Sociologist,* Vol. XXVIII, No. 2, December.

People's Conference against Globalisation. March 21–23, 2001. Delhi: Speaker's Hall, Constitution Club.

Perumpanani, Seelia Thomas. 2005. *History and Culture of Adivasis in Kerala [Keralathile Adivasikalute Jeevithavum Samskaravum* (Malayalam)*]*. Kottayam: Current Books.

Petras, James and Henry Veltmeyer. 2001. *Globalisation Unmasked*. Delhi: Madhyam Books.

Pinto, Ambrose S.J. 2000. *Indian Reality: Debt and Development*. Delhi: Indian Social Institute.

Prakash, B.A. (Ed.). 2004. *Kerala's Economic Development: Performance and Problems in the Post-Liberalisation Period* (second edition). New Delhi: Sage Publications.

Prakash, P.K. 2002. *Alienated Land: History and Politics of Adivasi Land Issue [Anyadheenappedunna Bhoomi: Adivasi Bhoomi Prasnattinte Charithravum Rashtriyavum* (Malayalam)*]*. Kozhikode: Jayachandran Suhrudsamgham.

Pulapre, Balakrishnan. 2003. Globalisation, Growth and Justice. *Economic and Political Weekly,* Vol. XXXVIII, No. 30, July 26, p. 3171.

Radhakrishnan, M.G. 2003. Tribal Cleft. *India Today*, March 10, pp. 40–41.

Raghav, Narsly. 2002. A Decade of Reforms: What Does it Mean for the Marginalised? *Vikalp-Alternatives*, Vol. X, No. 1.

Raj, Felix. 2005. Globalisation and Plight of the Tribals. *The Rally*, Vol. 8, No. 9, February.

Raj, K.N. 1985. New Economic Policy. *Mainstream*, Vol. XXIV, No. 15, December 14.

Rajendraprasad. 2001. Tribal Land and Agricultural Work (Malayalam). *Madhyam Weekly*, November 9.

Raju, E.T. 1995. *AIVE* (Malayalam). Wayanad: Fedina Hilda.

Raju, E.T. 1999. *Tribal Study [Penappattile Chettadiyar* (Malayalam)*]*. Wayanad: Fedina Publications.

——, 1995. AIVE (Malayalam). Wayanad, Fedina Hilda

Rama, P. 2001. *Confronting Commercialisation of Health Care* [Arogyamegalayude Vanijyavalkaranam (Malayalam)]. Kochi: Kerala Sastra Sahita Parishad.

Rao, Mohan J. 1997. *Globalisation, International Inequality and Development.* Bangalore: Indo-Dutch Management Society.

Rohini. 1994. Development/Welfare Programmes and Tribal Life Pattern. Kerala (Mimeo)

Roy, Arundhati. 2003. You Have Blood on Your Hands. *Frontline*, March 28, p. 45.

Roy, Chowdhury, Supriya. 2003. Old Classes and New Spaces: Urban Poverty, Unorganised Labour and New Unions. *Economic and Political Weekly*, Vol. XXXVIII, No. 50, December 13, pp. 5277–5284.

Sainath, P. 2004. Hope does Slowly in Wayanad. *The Hindu*, December 18.

——, 2004. The Cross and the Crisis. *The Hindu*, June 12.

Samal, Prasanna K. 1999. *Tracing the Linkages of Culture and Economy with the Development of Tribal Communities in Central Himalaya.* Bharatiya Samajik Chintan, XXIV, 1–4.

Scholte, Jan Aart. 1998. Globalisation: A New Imperialism? *Alumni Magazine*, pp. 11–13.

Seabrook, Jeremy. 2001. *Deccan Herald*, March 12.

Shah, Mihir. 2003. Nurseries of Alienation. *The Hindu*, December 30.

Sharma, Kalpana. 2003. Adivasis: The Forgotten. *The Hindu*, March 9.

Sheth, D.L. 2004. Globalisation and New Politics of Micro-Movements. *Economic and Political Weekly*, Vol. XXXIX, No. 1, January 3.

Singh, Ajith. 2002. *Mathrubhumi*, October 25.

Singh, K.S. 1994. *The Scheduled Tribes*. Delhi: Oxford University Press.

Singh, K. 1998. *A Citizen's Guide to the Globalisation of Finance*. Delhi: Madhyam Books.

Singh, Sanjay Kumar. 2001. *The Dark Clouds and the Silver Lining: Adivasi Struggle in Kerala*. Delhi: Kerala Study Group

Sreedevi, Jacob. 2003. A Bitter Brew in the High Ranges. *The Hindu*, *Sunday Magazine*, September 29.

Subramanya, R.K.A. 1996. *Social Aspect of Structural Adjustment in India*. New Delhi: Friedrich Ebert Stiftung.

Sundaram, G. 2003, Is This Globalisation? *The Hindu*. *Sunday Magazine*, February 2.

Sundaram, K. and Tendulkar, Suresh D. 2003. Poverty Among Social and Economic Groups in India in 1990s. *Economic and Political Weekly*, Vol. XXXVIII, No. 50, December 13, pp. 5263–76.

——, 2003. Poverty in India in the 1990s: An Analysis of Changes in 15 Major States. *Economic and Political Weekly*, Vol. XXXVIII, No.14, April 5, pp. 1385–93.

——, 2003. Poverty in India in the 1990s: Revised Results for All-India and 15 Major States of 1993–94. *Economic and Political Weekly*, Vol. XXXVIII, No. 46, November 15, pp. 4865–72.

Swaminathan, M.S. 2005. *The Hindu*, September 26.

Swamy, Dalip S. 1994. Delhi: Public Interest Research Group.

Teltumbde, Anand. 2000. *Globalisation and the Dalits*. www.ambedkar.org. Updated September, p. 5.

The Indigenous World 2001–2002. 2002. International World Group for Indigenous Affairs.

The International School of Dravidian Linguistics. 1996. *Land Alienation Encyclopedia of Dravidian Tribes*. Vol. 1, Trivandrum.

Thurston, E. 1987. *Castes and Tribes of Southern India*. Vol. II. New Delhi: J. Jetley for Asian Educational Services.

Tilak, Jandhyala B.G. 2004. Public Subsidies in Education in India. *Economic and Political Weekly*, Vol. XXXIX, No. 4, January 24, pp. 343–59.

Tirkey, Agapit, S.J. 2004. *Indigenous People and South Asian Jesuits*. Jivan, August.

Valavanal, Scaria. 2001. *Folk Medical Treatment [Nattarivu Chikitsamurakal (Malayalam)]*. Wayanad: Tudi Publications.

Varghese, K. George. 2003. Globalisation Traumas and New Social Imaginary: Visvakarma Community of Kerala. *Economic and Political Weekly*, Vol. XXXVIII, No. 45, November 8, pp. 4794–4801.

Varghese, Thomas. 2005. Perishing Agriculture and Declining Kerala. *Mathrubhumi*, October 31.

——, 2003. World Trade Agreement and Kerala Farmers. *Mathrubhumi*, September 15.

Velappan, K. 1994. *Tribals and Tribal Languages* (Malayalam). Trivandrum: The State Institute of Languages.

——, 2000. *Aborigines and Their Languages [Adivasikalum Adivasibhashakalum (Malayalam)]*. Thiruvananthapuram: The State Institute of Languages.

Voice. 1997. Adivasi Survey Report (Mimeo). Wayanad, December.

Index